FROM HIRE TO FIRE

& EVERYTHING IN BETWEEN

Managing the Employee Life Cycle –
Hire, Manage, Wellbeing & Exit

Natasha Hawker

Disclaimer

The material in this publication is in the nature of general comment about human resources issues only and does not represent professional advice (including legal advice). It is not intended to provide specific guidance for particular circumstances and it should not be relied on as the basis for any decision to take action or not to take action on any matter it covers. Readers should obtain professional advice where appropriate before making any such decision. The author and publisher disclaim all responsibility and liability to any person, arising directly or indirectly from any person taking or not taking action based on the information in this publication.

FROM HIRE TO FIRE & EVERYTHING IN BETWEEN

First published in Australia in 2014 by Natasha Hawker
Second Edition in Australia in 2018 by Natasha Hawker

© Natasha Hawker 2014 and 2018
The moral rights of the author have been asserted.

National Library of Australian Cataloguing-in-Publication entry

Author:	Hawker, Natasha, 1969 –
Title:	From Hire to Fire & Everything in Between / Natasha Hawker
ISBN:	978-0-9942073-1-9
Subjects:	Employee Management
	Management
	Human Resources
	Small Business

Dewey Number: 023.9

Author photo by Lauren Abi-Hanna – studiosolandco.com
Editorial services by Grammar Factory
Cover by Julia Kuris – Designerbility
Internal Design by Charlotte Gelin – Charlotte Gelin Design
Printed in Australia by Minuteman Press Prahran 63871

Dedicated to
Mark, Amberley, Jamie and Benjamin

TESTIMONIALS

'There is no doubt that managing people is the hardest part of running a small business. It is complicated, challenging and changing – which generally means it ends up in the too hard basket. Natasha Hawker has written a book to demystify managing people, and delivered it in a way that makes sense, it is hugely practical, and a must read for any business owner.'

Andrew Griffiths
Australia's #1 Small Business and Entrepreneurial Author

'We have worked with over 4500 small- and medium-sized businesses within Australia and overseas. There is not one of those businesses that either has not had, or is not currently having, some form of team issues. The Hire to Fire and Everything in Between book is the only book of its kind that truly gives owners and managers of businesses not only the practical and simple steps of what to do, but also the confidence and certainty that they are making the right moves.

This book is a reference book that should be within reach of every business owner/mid-market Leader as it is a reference for them to consistently refer to, to make sure they are on track, doing the right things and are compliant.

This is a must have tool that owners and leaders should have at the ready.'

David Dugan – Abundance Global

'Natasha is an expert in employee matters. What she doesn't know about hiring, managing and firing isn't worth knowing. More importantly, she can show you how to effectively engage, motivate and direct your team to make your business a success.'

Glen Carlson
Co-founder and Global Director – Dent Global

'Natasha really knows her stuff and I have an immense respect for her, both as a human resources practitioner, and also as a successful, energetic and engaging architect of her own ever-growing business.

I have been lucky enough to attend a number of Employee Matters events and have also worked with most members of the Employee Matters team. Every interaction I have with Natasha and her team reinforces my confidence in their exceptional skills in the field of human resources management. My trust in their ability and skill is such that I have frequently referred my own clients, friends and family.

Natasha's willingness to impart what she knows reflects her true generosity of spirit. This book is a brain-dump of epic proportions, and we are all lucky that Natasha has taken the time to put her years of experience and expertise onto paper and share it with us all.'

Danny King
Principal Solicitor – DK Legal

'Within these pages you will find the solution to most of the issues you've encountered, when managing your team. People management doesn't have to remain a mystery and it doesn't have to be hard! Now you can tap into the extensive and practical expertise Natasha has generously shared in this book, you no longer need to be afraid of getting it wrong. Instead, you can enjoy the many benefits of having a talented, engaged and productive team – the same benefits Natasha brings to her clients.'

Susan Rochester
Director – Balance at Work

'Natasha Hawker from Employee Matters is a human resources angel to watch over your business. Her experience, knowledge and expertise in the field of hiring, managing and firing employees, while protecting your business throughout every stage, is second to none. I highly recommend any business to engage and learn from Natasha Hawker.'

Justine Coombe
Founder & CEO of Ignite Digital

'As a small business owner for the past ten years, I know how challenging managing a team of employees can be. Especially in a fast-growing business. Attracting the best talent and maintaining team stability is particularly demanding – but also keeping up with the ever-changing employment relations legislation!

Natasha understands small business and their challenges but brings her extensive corporate experience to small business in a way that makes commercial sense. She understands my business and provides solid guidance and support – from team productivity to succession planning. This is a must read for anyone running a small business.'

Anne-Marie Sparrow
Managing Director – Cube

'The demands on small- and medium-size businesses are challenging. As a business owner, you need to focus your energies on the critical areas to establish and compete in the market. However, you are also competing for the most important aspect of your success against large, medium and other small businesses – your team. You have to attract, grow, motivate and reward your team, and this fight for the best possible people extends well beyond your products, markets and even geographies.

Our business has been extremely lucky as we are able to draw on Natasha's (and her team's) skills, knowledge and experience to support us in this challenge. As a smaller business, access to this expertise can only come through the choice of the correct partner and Natasha understands our business and how we operate and is therefore a natural extension in helping us succeed.'

Steve Orleow
Former Director / General Manager – BioPak

'Being a small- to medium-size business, issues around human resources is one of those black holes that only seem to grow larger and larger as the world gets ever more complicated. Natasha has rare skills that allow her to encapsulate and effectively communicate potential symptoms and risks around employee and organisational behaviour, which allows small businesses to sleep better at night.'

Stephen Tamas
Director – Seed Outsourcing

CONTENTS

FOREWORD   15

ACKNOWLEDGEMENTS   17

WHY SHOULD YOU CARE?   23

Do I have your attention now?   25
So, what's next?   27

PART 1: HIRE

Uh oh – I think I need some help!   **33**

How do you know it's time to grow your team?   34
Who do you need, and how can you organise them?   36
Phase 1 – Organisation charts   36
Phase 2 – Job descriptions   39
Phase 3 – Transition plan   39

What type of employees do I need?   **41**

Permanent employment   41
Casual employment   43
Fixed-term/fixed-task employment   45
Non-employees such as independent contractors   46
Labour-hire workers (otherwise referred to as temps)   48
Volunteers   48
Which is right for you?   48

The foundations – what you need to know before hiring anyone   **53**

Modern Awards   53
Fair Work Australia National Employment Standards   55
Enterprise bargaining   61
Protection from Unfair Dismissal   61
Insurance   61

Superannuation 75

Checklist – What I need before I hire 77

Finding the perfect match **79**

Step 1 – Determine your job vacancies 79

Step 2 – Recruitment approvals 79

Step 3 – Prepare the job briefs 80

Step 4 – Advertising 81

Step 5 – Candidate communication 81

Step 6 – Interviews 82

Step 7 – Identity, reference, background and visa checks 88

Making the offer – how to get them to say 'I do' **103**

The letter of offer 103

The employment contract 105

What to include in an offer of employment 106

PART 2: MANAGE

From good to great – organisational development **111**

Phase 1 – Organisation charts 111

Phase 2 – Job descriptions 114

Phase 3 – Transition plan 116

Phase 4 – Managing the transition 118

'First Rule of Leadership: everything is your fault' – A bug's life **123**

What type of leader are you? 124

What makes a good leader? 126

Are there times when leadership is particularly important? 128

How can I improve my leadership skills? 128

Policy – Setting the standards for employee management **131**

Structure of a policy 133

Which policies do I need? 133

Storing your policies 134

Usage 135

Review 135

What if things go wrong? 137

Training – To build great teams you need to invest in your people 139

Induction and orientation 139

Training in company policies 141

Ongoing skill development in the workplace 145

Engagement – Want an extra 20% profit this year? 153

1. Company identity 155

2. People 158

3. Leadership 170

The results of a great culture 171

Leave 177

Long service leave 177

Parental leave 178

Community service leave (including jury duty) 180

Domestic Violence Leave 182

Wellbeing – How to stay compliant and have healthy employees 183

Where should I begin with safety? 185

Your responsibilities 188

Provide information, training and instruction to
all employees 192

The last word – the safety efforts of most businesses are insufficient 194

Performance management 197

Strategies for managing performance 197

Conducting a performance meeting 199

Performance management FAQs 202

Performance management and annual reviews 206

The golden rule – be consistent 207

It all comes down to communication   211

Creating your communications strategy   212
Planning your communication   213
Ways of communicating   214
Having the difficult conversation   224
45% of communication is listening   226
What to put in writing   227

Measurement – why bother?   229

What to measure   230
How and when to measure?   234
What are the benefits of measurement?   243

PART 3: EXIT

Resignation   249

Verbal resignation   249
Written resignation   250
Counter offers   251
Communication   252
Handover   253
Farewell   254

Redundancy   255

How much do you need to pay?   256
Keep the future in mind   257

Exiting   259

Exiting for inappropriate behaviour   259
Exiting for fraud or theft   261

Death   269

Exit interviews   **271**

What to ask in an exit interview   273

Alumni   **277**

How to create an alumni program: 278

What's next?   **279**

Phase 1 – Organisation charts   279
Phase 2 – Job descriptions   279
Phase 3 – Transition plan   280

CONCLUSION   281

RESOURCES   285

Sample interview questions   **285**

Technical – Can they do the job?
What skills are they bringing to the role?   285
Behavioural – How do they work?   287
Cultural – Are they likely to be a cultural fit to the organisation?   288
Probing – Can you get more information?   288
Questions to avoid   289

Sample policies   **291**

Annual leave   291
WHS Policy 1 – Master Workplace Health and Safety Policy   293
WHS Policy 2 – Safety Duty Holders   296
WHS safe operating procedure – Safety Duty Holders   299

REFERENCES   301
GLOSSARY   303

FOREWORD

by Angela Vithoulkas
CEO VIVO CAFÉ GROUP
Small Business Owner & Advocate

I have been a business owner for over three decades, buying, selling and designing cafes. I have met and collaborated with many other business owners and no matter which one of us you talk to, regardless of where we are in the cycle of our business, we all have the same challenge – our employees.

My very full business life leaves me little down time, time I consider precious and irreplaceable. When Natasha told me she was writing a book, I told her I couldn't wait to read it and that I would **make** the time. I have worked with Natasha on a number of occasions, even interviewed her myself, and I have always been impressed with her down to earth knowledge of the reality of being a business owner and managing a team. That's why I knew reading her book would be worth it.

I clearly don't serve every customer in my businesses, and without great employees working as a team, I wouldn't have the successful businesses that I have been fortunate to be part of. I'm also in an industry notorious for short-term employment and poor team cohesiveness. It can be the death of a business when your people and you as the owner are pulling in separate directions. To create a great work environment, that people want to be a part of – including the employer, you must value each other. Natasha talks about this and the direct correlation to increase in productivity when people 'go that extra mile'.

Hiring and firing people can be some of your most defining moments as an employer; you are making a decision based on some information given to you and your 'gut feel'. But the hard part starts at hiring and all the details around it – and the responsibilities that it comes with – this information is rarely given out, or in your business plan, until now. Natasha has put together a fabulous, well written and easy to understand book that will give you some 'ah ha' moments and explain what some things really mean, like 'casual versus permanent employment', 'pro rata on annual leave' and what are your risks and possibility of penalties.

Hiring someone comes with responsibilities of making sure you meet your legal obligations, create a safe working environment and really do your homework on who is about to enter and be part of life for you, your team and your business. Some of us think hiring stops at the interview and reading the CV, but the serious detail is in the follow up; Natasha takes you through that step by step.

Firing, resignations and terminations are also a huge challenge for the employer. It can leave you exposed financially and emotionally affect your team morale. At some point you will most likely have to do this for almost every employee you have – for some it will be amicable and voluntary, for others not so much. Wouldn't it be great to have someone to help you through this? Natasha's book is thorough and no-nonsense where it deals with this subject.

From Hire to Fire and Everything in Between should come with your ABN, as a handout, and I wouldn't be surprised to see well-worn copies on the desk of many employers. I wish this book was around when I started in business, it would have saved me a lot of heartache.

ACKNOWLEDGEMENTS

I would like to start by thanking all the wonderful people that I have worked with over the years. I am particularly grateful for the twelve years I had at Accenture, where every day I was exposed to HR best practice.

I would also like to thank all of my Employee Matters clients for trusting us to help you with one of your most prized possessions – your business.

I very much want to acknowledge some of the colleagues who helped me with the more technical 'know how' to write chapters on the factors that impact small businesses on a daily basis. They are:

- **Jacqui Pretty**, my editor for her expertise, patience and for making me look good twice now. You made me an author – thank you, Jacqui.

- **Andrew Griffiths**, my book mentor. If someone had told me at school that I would write a book in 2014 and complete a second edition in 2018, I would have said they were nuts. You have made this possible with your willingness to share your knowledge, your simple and clear explanations, your endless encouragement and your belief in me. This has all been surrounded with your wonderful sense of humour – thank you!

- **Jason Alison** from IPAR, who helped me with the latest developments around WorkCover. Jason is a really busy guy and I am so grateful for his time, experience and insights. This reinforced that he really does care for small businesses and their challenges.

- **Chris Talbot** who, with his wife, runs a Financial Planning and Legal practice, and is a whiz with numbers. Chris helped me think through the employee metrics that can really help small businesses – thank you for giving so generously of your knowledge.

- **Ian Till** from People Measures, who is a guru in the leadership space.

- **Ben Walker** from Inspire CA who has been our life-changing accountant, and who has educated, protected and encouraged me to get to know my numbers and even enjoy them. Plus, he is an expert on everything superannuation.

- **Steven Sams**, who is a WHS expert and has been an amazing supporter of Employee Matters and me. There is not much he doesn't know about WH&S and what I really admire about him is that he comes from a place of having personal experience with a serious workplace injury so he 'gets' both sides.

- **Rebecca Fleming** from Gow Gates. I met Rebecca about eight years ago and she helped us navigate the insurance minefield with her wealth of knowledge from over twenty-five years' experience. What I love most about Rebecca is the enthusiasm and interest that she shares for your business.

- **Patrick Vanderham** from Hemisphere Migration who has shared his ten years of expertise and his wisdom around the recent changes around migration and visas.

- **David Braidwood** (my Dad), without whom this book would not have been finished and for his unwavering support and interest and also his proofreading.

- **Caroline Ross**, my right hand in New Zealand. As always, Caroline was there with support and encouragement and her brilliant research skills. Thank you, Carly, for always being willing to have a go and for finding the facts for me.

- **Paul Ackerman**, one of our fabulous senior Employee Experts who was updating pieces of content and fact checking for me. We are thrilled to have you on the team.

- **David Brown**, our GM and my other right hand for so many things. Mainly getting me to pick a launch date and just start re-writing but also for his unwavering support and encouragement, as well as, helping me update the content.

- **Julia Kuris**, from Designerbility who designed the fabulous book cover.

- **Charlotte Gelin**, for the sparkling interior design work and making the book so readable.

- **Mark Hawker**, my husband and business partner who has always been and will always be my editor. Thank you for proofreading while juggling the kids and the business. I am incredibly lucky to have found you and your unwavering support for me cannot be matched.

I would like to thank the wonderful team at Employee Matters; we are so lucky to have you all and so are our clients. Your enthusiasm for our clients and for delivering great work is second to none.

I am very lucky to be surrounded by the most amazing bunch of friends, especially my wonderful girlfriends, some of whom I have known since high school. Thank you for your support, love and laughter and for bearing with me while I hibernated to write this book first and second time around.

To my extended family – Meryl and David (Mum and Dad), Tiffany (the best sister in the world) and her husband Rufino, and Mark and Brooke (my brother and his partner) – thank you for all your encouragement and support. Especially to Mum and Dad for religiously asking, 'What's the word count today?' And for bringing me up with the attitude that if you work hard it will eventually pay off. I was lucky to have an amazing father-in-law, Laurie, who has since passed and was ill at the time of writing my first edition, but he still bubbled with enthusiasm and wanted to know how he could help. He would be so chuffed to see the updated edition.

I am blessed to have three wonderful kids who showed amazing interest in the books and were patient when I was spending so much time locked away writing, making me tea and meals. Amberley, Jamie and Benjamin, you are the best! This book is for you and I hope that you too will set big goals and dream big.

Finally, to my rock and my first editor Mark – thank you for your patience in correcting all my grammar errors. You are the love of my life and my business partner. You support me and my dreams and keep the family running smoothly. Thank you for all your love, support and encouragement.

'Companies die because their managers focus on the economic activity of producing goods and services and forget that their organisations' true nature is that of a community of humans.'

ARIE DE GUES, THE LIVING COMPANY

WHY SHOULD YOU CARE?

Many business owners start their businesses because they have a great idea that they wish to take to market or they are really good at something technical. People very rarely start a business because they want to manage employees.

If business goes well, however, then you're likely to end up with employees sooner or later. The bad news is that I can absolutely guarantee that if you have employees, you are going to have an issue at some point. It's a numbers game – the longer you are in business and the more employees you have, the greater the chance of internal conflicts, performance management issues or harassment.

And then what? If you're like most small business owners, you're probably ill-equipped to deal with these issues.

Because small business owners generally get into business to launch an idea or leverage their technical skills, they resist learning about employee recruitment, management and dismissal. It all seems too complicated and with legislation changing all the time it feels impossible to keep up. This leads some owners to bury their heads in the sand, thinking that what they don't know won't hurt them.

I'm afraid, though, that lacking knowledge or experience is not a defence. Claiming ignorance and taking a 'she'll be right, mate' attitude will not help you if you are called before the Fair Work Commissioner. As an employer, you are expected to know the legislation.

This lack of detailed knowledge is not just an issue with small businesses; it is also prevalent in mid-size businesses. There is often, at this level, a dependence on information that is out of date, such as the idea that to terminate an employee is fine, as long as you have given them two verbal warnings and a written one. This is definitely not the case.

The other issue I commonly see is working around the expense of employees. As many businesses start on a shoestring, they often look for cheaper employment options, like using cash-in-hand employees or independent contractors. This could cost you more in the long run with the Australian Taxation Office (ATO) regularly reviewing industry segments for cash employees and charging significant fines for this activity. While using independent contractors may feel like a simpler arrangement, if they are acting as permanent employees, this is a breach known as *sham contracting*, an area that has been a focus of the Fair Work Ombudsman and the ATO in recent times.

Others trying to avoid the complications of hiring, taking the approach of a handshake or verbal agreement. The issue here is that once you have an employee completing an activity in exchange for cash, the legal view is that an employment relationship has been established, regardless of whether or not there's a written contract. As such, the arrangement falls under all the legal requirements of an employer-employee relationship and all the same legislation applies.

In one sense it's understandable – sometimes having employees is simply a means to an end so, of course, you want the process to be as simple as possible. The challenge with this approach is that, if you don't get it right from the beginning, you are likely to be drawn into more frequent and time-consuming interactions and processes later. In short, the less time and effort you put into your employees, the more open you leave your business for problems to arise.

At the mid-size level, we find that many are not aware of, nor are they compliant with, their Modern Award obligations with many businesses breaching their Awards by not paying the correct rate of pay or adhering to their requirement to consult on major workplace change.

Not having legally compliant processes in place, or worse still, having *nothing* in place can be very expensive. One example is the area of Modern Awards, which set out all the terms and conditions governing an industry or occupation. There are some very large financial implications for getting this wrong, with each breach of a Modern Award exposing your business to fines of up to $63,000 for a corporation and $12, 600 for an individual. Let me be very clear here – this is *per breach*. A breach can be as simple as not giving out the Fair Work Information Statement to every new permanent employee. Worse still, if Fair Work senses there may be a breach, or multiple breaches, they can enter your business and conduct a complete audit. Please note that these fines are reviewed regularly and may have increased since this book was initially published.

The reality is that having employees and managing the relationship with them can be complex, but it is part of being a business owner. And not abiding by the legislation has serious consequences.

Do I have your attention now?

Good, because beyond financial disincentives, there are even more important reasons for getting your employee-related processes right.

First, employees can make or break a business, so it is critical to get this right. According to CEB in the webinar *Breakthrough Performance in the New Work Environment 2013*, 'To date, business performance gains have come from better labour efficiency and companies getting more and more from their investment in employees.' If you're in the majority of businesses that are looking for growth, then effective employee management is essential.

Managing employees also gives you the opportunity to become a great leader. In *Creating the Best Workplace on Earth*, a three-year study completed by Rob Coffee and Gareth Jones for *Harvard Business Review* in May 2013, it was found that employees, 'will not follow a leader they feel is inauthentic', therefore, by becoming an authentic leader you will be able to motivate and inspire your team to give you their best effort, which, in turn will help you achieve your business goals.

Additionally, having the correct processes in place means you can:

- Attract and retain the best employees,
- Maximise productivity,
- Grow quickly, and
- Boost your brand's and your business's reputation.

This will give you certainty and confidence, because you will have the tools to tackle any employee issues. What typically happens in a business where there is limited structure and processes is that rules and outcomes tend to be decided reactively. The risk with this is that, very quickly, employees will feel that there is inconsistency and become unsettled. According to research conducted by John Halliwell from the University of British Columbia and Haifeng Huang from the University of Alberta, employees were seen to be significantly happier in environments where they ranked management trustworthiness highly, so it is important to get this right.

Finally, if you care about your employees you'll simply want to do the right thing by them. In the interviews completed in preparation for writing this book it became really clear to me that these business owners really cared about their teams and the individuals within their teams. When a leader is coming from this space they will intrinsically try to not only do the right thing for the business, but also the right thing for the employee – a win-win scenario.

So, what's next?

You might be thinking, 'I hear what you're saying, and I understand how important this is, but it still feels really complicated.'

The good news is that, with education and preparation, you can manage all of these issues. This book will teach you how.

I've written this book specifically for business owners who don't have the time to go wading through the vast sea of information out there, and who might not have the budget to outsource this part of their businesses. Or they realise they need to know how to hire a great HR resource. Instead, *From Hire to Fire* will be your handbook, with practical advice and frameworks for hiring employees, firing employees (gulp!) and everything in between.

From Hire to Fire has three sections that cover the life cycle of your employees:

- Hire
- Manage
- Exit

Hire

In this section you will learn how to figure out whether your business is ready to support employees, as well as the type of employee that will best suit your requirements. This will help you avoid a claim of sham contracting from Fair Work or the ATO. In addition, this will enable you to develop a flexible workforce and help you manage your costs as well as the persistent peaks and troughs of business.

You will also learn about the legal foundations you need to have in place before hiring anyone, including Modern Awards, insurance, superannuation, your Workplace Health and Safety obligations and more.

Finally, you will learn techniques to ensure that your preferred candidate accepts *your* job offer, and not one from your competitors.

Manage

Here you will learn how to be a great leader. I will cover how to build a business that attracts and retains the best employees, including how to develop a highly motivated and productive team. I will also explain which policies you must have in place to be compliant with the legislation so that you, your business and your employees are all protected.

You will also learn how to navigate the legal minefield of performance management.

Exit

Finally, you will learn about the various ways people may leave your business and how you should respond to these situations to remain compliant.

You'll learn what to do when your best employee resigns and what you can do to encourage them to reverse their decision, keeping everyone happy.

I will also cover how to reduce the risks of being sued when exiting someone from your business. This is a skill that I believe all business owners must have to run their businesses effectively. Large corporates might be able to operate effectively despite non-performers, but this is extremely damaging for small to medium enterprises. This is particularly important when one non-performing employee might be 10% or 20% of your workforce.

My vision for this book (it sits on a Post-It note on my desk as I type) is for it to become a dog-eared employee 'bible' that lives on your desk. It will give you the confidence to make decisions and implement processes, referring to it as needed. Let's say you need to have a performance management conversation, or you want to hire the best employees, or you are about to instigate a major change in the workplace and, maybe unlike other attempts, you want this one to stick. That's when you can refer to this book.

From your perspective, it will help you tackle anything employee-related with confidence and rigour.

From your employees' perspective, they will love the structure, fairness and sense of order and purpose these processes bring to your business. They will believe you care for them and, as a result, they will give you higher levels of discretionary effort, leading to increased productivity and profitability for your business. And, let's face it, isn't that what every business owner in Australia wants?

PART 1: HIRE

UH OH – I THINK I NEED SOME HELP!

Orders are starting to pick up and your clients are as excited about your business as you are. You are running hard but there are only twenty-four hours in a day. You are starting to see some errors creeping in and you are concerned that if you muck up another order or leave it too much longer to get back to your client, your business will quickly start to decline. You know that your reputation is critical.

From a mid-size perspective, your wits and tenacity have got you this far, but you are not sure whether you are fully compliant with your legal requirements, nor do you think you are hiring the best that you can afford or getting the most productivity out of your employees.

It might be time to bring on some extra help. But how? You really never wanted to employ people and be the boss. What if you're not a great boss? You don't understand the employment relations legislation, you really dislike interviewing, and you're worried about making the wrong decision. Essentially, you feel that *with employees come issues.*

You wonder whether you should continue flying solo, but you know there are ramifications if you do, mostly around the ability to grow past a certain point.

Growing and succeeding in business with a team will be one of the most challenging and rewarding journeys you will ever have. I liken it to having a baby. The idea seems great at the time of conception, and then you experience pregnancy which, whether it's blissful or horrendous, can be long and uncomfortable. The birth can be challenging, but what a reward. Then you get sleepless nights and no smiles or gratitude. Then when your baby smiles or giggles at you – wow, there's nothing like it. Next comes the toddler phase – where you are constantly chasing and dealing with tantrums. Then comes structure with the start of preschool or school, and then, *finally*, growth and reward.

How do you know it's time to grow your team?

So how do you know whether now's the time to grow your team? It's important to look at your business. Can you afford an employee, and what are the alternatives if you can't?

1. Start by forecasting your revenue targets for the next twelve months. If you already have a business plan, this will be as simple as looking at your existing targets. If you *don't* have a business plan, download a template to get started at: business.gov.au/Planning/Templates-and-tools/Business-Plan-Template-and-Guide

2. Grab a piece of paper and write down everything that you currently do over a week (yes, *everything*), and allocate a time to it. How long does it usually take you to complete a particular task? Once you have completed this, leave it for a day or two and then come back to it; you will discover even more tasks that you had forgotten.

3. Group similar tasks into categories such as social media, finance, technology and business development.

4. Now it is going to get hard – really hard! It's time for some honest reflection – what are you good at? What are your strengths and what do you need to focus on to grow your business? What could someone do better or quicker than you? Part of the challenge of being an entrepreneur is being able to turn your hand to most things, given time, but this may not be the best use of your skills or your time. Put a red circle around these particular tasks – did you halve the list? If not, try again.

5. With the list of tasks that you are comfortable to give away, think about the people around you who may be able to help. One of my friends worked free for me for a couple of months out of Dubai because she believed in me and my business. So, are there any people in your network that might volunteer? If you start with volunteers, even friends and family, remember not to take advantage of them. As soon as we could afford to, I took my friend to an expensive lunch to thank her for her work and support (and she is now an ongoing key member of my team). Starting with a couple of volunteers might help confirm or test whether your business is at a point where you can sustain employees. This will also force you to structure roles and processes to deliver your product or service.

Once you have decided which tasks you can reassign, think about how many hours this will free up for you. You can then look to spend this time on work activities that will bring more revenue into the business. It is important to forecast the amount of revenue you can generate now you have additional time. If you can cover the salary of an employee with this expected revenue, then it is definitely time to hire.

When you are looking to grow a business, it is important that you start with your end game in mind as this will drive many of the early decisions that you make. By end game I mean – what is your intention for your business? Is it to sell in three years? Is it to hand it on to your children? Or is this your gig until retirement, when you plan to sell and sail around the world? For example, we have a client who has a landscaping and garden maintenance business with about six employees. He is looking at growth opportunities in building maintenance, but he also knows that ultimately, he does not want to work very hard. The challenge for him is that his business is a low-margin business, so he needs the economies of scale that come with a growth in headcount to drive up revenue and profit. As a result, he is looking to increase his employee numbers alongside client numbers to achieve his objectives.

Who do you need, and how can you organise them?

If you've decided it's time to grow your team, don't rush to Seek or Indeed just yet! First you need to consider how your business will grow, and how these new roles can support that growth.

Businesses evolve over time and, in small business, this growth is typically reactive rather than proactive. Do you agree? If you asked most business owners whether their business looks as they expected it to when they started it, most would answer no. It is more likely that you won a huge piece of work and you realised that you suddenly needed an employee, or two, or an entire team.

Organisational design is an area that large corporates spend a considerable amount of time and money getting right and it is a continuous process. I believe that if businesses spent more time on this area they would reap many benefits. After all, it is essential that all the components of your business are working cohesively to achieve your ultimate outcome. Otherwise the risk is waste, missed opportunities, increased costs and inefficiencies.

Planning your organisation

Phase 1 – Organisation charts

1. Draw your ideal organisation chart. Who will sit where, who will report to whom and what will their titles and levels of responsibility be? Does your plan make sense? Or is it still based on the original business you started three years ago? If you only have your original or a very dated chart, draw up your current organisation chart. It might look something like this:

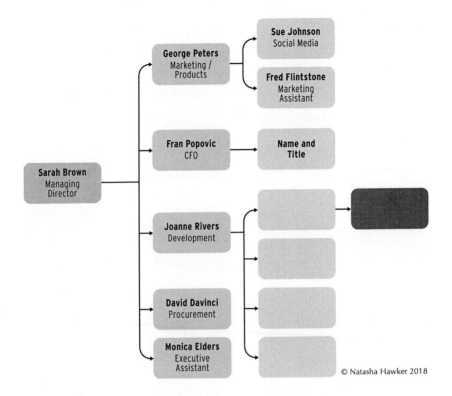

© Natasha Hawker 2018

2. Now think about your business plan and forecast how your business might need to look to service your future clients. Think forward twelve months or two years. What do you expect to be some of the technological, product, skills or opportunity impacts? How will this affect your team and resourcing requirements?

Consider completing a SWOT analysis for your business at this point. A SWOT analysis enables you to review your current or future strengths, weaknesses, opportunities and threats. If you have not done one before, use the following grid as a guide. For this exercise, let your mind roam. Just list all strengths, weaknesses, opportunities (these can just be ideas) and potential or real threats to your business. Once you have answered these questions, you can use this SWOT analysis to develop strategies for achieving your business goals and generating contingency plans, including hiring new employees. This exercise can be very revealing.

STRENGTHS	WEAKNESSES
• What advantages does your business have?	• What disadvantages does your business have?
• What do you do better than anyone else?	• What could you improve?
• What factors mean that you get the sale?	• What should you avoid?
• What is your business's Unique Selling Proposition?	• What factors lose you sales?

OPPORTUNITIES	THREATS
• What good opportunities can you spot?	• What obstacles do you face?
• What interesting trends are you aware of?	• What are your competitors doing?
• What changes in the market or industry can be used to benefit your business?	• What changes in the market or industry may have a negative impact on your business?
• What gaps or needs in the market can you fulfil?	• Do you have bad debt or cash-flow problems?

3. The next step is to compare the two organisation charts – are there any glaring omissions or opportunities to merge roles? Is one area top heavy, or over- or under-resourced? Are there opportunities for developing certain roles with multiple skills so they can cover other roles? This will reduce your exposure to attrition and enable you to effectively cover your annual leave schedule. This will also address the development desires of your employees and minimise financial impacts to the business.

4. Now you have your road map for the changes you may need to make to the business over the next six to twelve months. Once this is clear, it will make it easier to work towards your goals.

Phase 2 – Job descriptions

1. Draft job descriptions based on the roles in your organisation chart, including the tasks you listed under the *Part 1 Hire chapter – How do you know it's time to grow your team?*

2. Review all the job descriptions you've written. Will these roles work logically and cohesively, or do you need to make further adjustments? Are there any gaps in task responsibilities or missing links between roles?

Phase 3 – Transition plan

1. Review the current state and future state of your business and plan how you will transition over time to the future state.

2. Conduct quarterly reviews against your transition plan to check on progress and adjust as required.

Now that you're clearer on the positions you need to fill and how they fit into your organisational plan, it's time to consider which type of employees you need – permanent, casual, fixed-term, independent contractors, temps or volunteers.

WHAT TYPE OF EMPLOYEES DO I NEED?

If you've decided it's time to grow your team, the next question is what type of employees you actually need to meet your requirements. Your choices are permanent full-time, permanent part-time, casual employment, fixed-term/fixed-task employment, independent contractors, labour-hire workers and volunteers. Who knew there was so much to choose from?

Do you get a full-time employee because you easily have enough work to keep another person occupied five days a week, or do you choose someone casual until the workflow is steadier? Beyond the amount of work you have to delegate, the type of employees that you hire will have legal ramifications that you must be prepared to manage before you even start advertising for your first role.

Permanent employment

Permanent employees may work full-time or part-time.

The proportion of full-time employees decreased from 70.6% in August 2008 to 67.6% in August 2017 (Australian Bureau of Statistics).

According to fairwork.gov.au, a part-time employee:

- Works, on average, less than 38 hours per week
- Usually works regular hours each week
- Is entitled to the same benefits as a full-time employee, but on a pro rata basis
- Is a permanent employee or on a fixed-term contract

A full-time employee has ongoing employment and works, on average, around 38 hours each week. The actual hours of work for an employee in a particular job or industry are agreed between the employer and the employee and/or set by an Award or Registered Agreement. (fairwork.gov.au)

Permanent part-time employees are different to casual employees in that they typically work the same hours each week and these hours are reasonably predictable.

Whether full-time or part-time, permanent employees receive benefits such as overtime, annual leave, long service leave, paid personal leave, payment for jury duty and payment for public holidays. Overtime payment amounts are covered in the relevant Award (see *The foundations* for more information on this) and some Awards allow for a time in lieu arrangement. Time in lieu is where any additional hours above and beyond the normal hours worked are recorded and then the additional time is taken as leave with pay at a mutually convenient time by the employee.

All permanent employees in Australia are entitled to four weeks' annual leave per year under the minimum conditions. This is accrued monthly and you can't pay out leave in cash unless you are terminating the employment, where any accrued leave not yet taken is paid out at this point. Where employees are part-time, they receive their annual leave entitlements on a pro rata basis.

An employer can only direct an employee to take annual leave in some situations. For example, when:

- The business is closed during the Christmas and New Year period
- An employee has accumulated excess annual leave

The rules about when and if an employer can direct an employee to take annual leave is set out in Awards and Registered Agreements. (fairwork.gov.au/leave/annual-leave/directing-an-employee-to-take-annual-leave)

Once you hire a permanent or casual employee, remember to give them the Fair Work Information sheet (which you can find at fairwork. gov.au/employment/fair-work-information-statement/pages/default. aspx). This will ensure you meet your obligations under the FWA.

When it comes to dismissal, these workers generally have access to the complete range of legal remedies. Damages awarded to a permanent employee would typically be higher than those awarded to a casual or fixed-term employee.

Casual employment

Although casual employees offer your business more flexibility, this type of employment can be more complex to understand because some aspects are the same as permanent employees while others are different.

Casual workers work on an as-needs basis, with an irregular pattern of work. Each time the casual works, it is deemed that they are entering into a distinct and separate contract. Practically, casual work involves employment for fewer hours than the normal, full-time working week, and it's normal for casuals to be paid by the hour.

Casual employees receive no accruals of permanent employee benefits such as overtime, annual leave, long service leave, paid personal (sick) leave or payment for public holidays. Their rate of pay does, however, incorporate a loading to compensate for the lack of benefits. This is currently 25% on top of their base rate of pay.

Casuals are generally not entitled to long service leave, but check the relevant state legislation. Casuals are entitled to unpaid community service leave, but they are not entitled to paid jury service leave. Be aware that for some roles, after a casual has worked on a regular and systematic basis for a set period of time, they are required to be offered full-time or part-time permanent employment.

When we started Employee Matters, we had no idea what the levels of work were going to be, although we knew that we wanted to have employees. We started by using casual employees as the work was irregular and there was no firm indication of future work. This enabled us to start our business in a very cost-effective manner.

Casuals have less protection when it comes to dismissal; they are not protected under Unfair Dismissal laws unless they have completed a minimum period of twelve months of service and all casuals are excluded from minimum notice periods. Unless their relevant Award, employment contract or enterprise agreement states otherwise, casual employees can be dismissed at the end of their shift. The rationale for this is that they are typically employed from shift to shift.

If you need to dismiss a casual employee and they are not exempt from Unfair Dismissal laws, as with permanent employees you need to use procedural fairness, including giving a valid reason for the dismissal. Casual employees who are excluded from Unfair Dismissal could still be able to bring a claim under general protection if dismissed for a prescribed reason, such as a workplace right discrimination, a breach of contract, Award or agreement or a trade practices claim. They could also claim that they were, in fact, a permanent employee.

Review your casual employees' contracts prior to their six-month employment anniversary, or twelve-month anniversary for small business employees. If a casual has been working on a 'regular and systematic basis' for at least six months and has a reasonable expectation of continuing work on this basis, then they will have access to Unfair Dismissal remedies. Even if there has been a short break in their employment (typically less than three months), the employee will be able to bring an Unfair Dismissal claim if the total period of employment is at least twelve months.

Fixed-term/fixed-task employment

A fixed-task employee is typically hired for the duration of a project or range of tasks. This means the fixed-term employee is employed on a contract with a specified end date. The end date is mutually agreed prior to the employee starting work. On that date, the contract comes to an end and the employee is terminated. There is no need for either party to terminate the contract because it is automatic; there is no need for a resignation or dismissal. These contracts can be useful when you are covering a permanent employee's parental leave, or when you are not sure if there will be enough work at the end of the contract.

Generally fixed-term employees and fixed-task employees are excluded from:

- Unfair Dismissal provisions under section 386 of the FWA

- Minimum notice of termination

- Redundancy pay

- Employers having to notify and consult with unions before implementing redundancies in the workplace.

Fixed-term employees are entitled to all other leave provisions, such as annual and personal leave, on a pro rata basis. For example, if you have a fixed-term employee for six months, then they are entitled to two weeks of annual leave and five days of personal leave. That is, half the entitlements that a permanent employee would receive over twelve months.

As a business owner it's a good idea to include a notice provision, which will allow either party to terminate the contract prior to the specified termination date, without the other party being able to claim a breach of contract, meaning there will be no damages to claim. In this case, the compensation likely to be awarded will be what the employee would have received if the contract had continued to the agreed termination date. However, the disadvantage of this provision is that it will generally prevent the contract from falling within the federal Unfair Dismissal exclusion.

Workers may be able to perform a number of concurrent fixed-term contracts or fixed-task contracts; however, you need to take care to ensure that case law does not determine these contracts warrant treatment as a permanent employee. To ascertain this, it is best to speak with an employee expert or an employment lawyer.

Non-employees such as independent contractors

An independent contractor is someone who contracts their labour to a business and would typically use their own equipment for a specified purpose, but they remain separate to the principal and are not strictly part of the business.

The relationship between a contractor and a principal generally comes to an end at the completion of a task. The contract does not have any provisions for annual leave, personal leave, compassionate leave or other statutory entitlements that an employer-employee relationship would include.

A key point of difference between an employee and an independent contractor is that the contractor has the right to exercise or control the manner in which the work is performed, including the place of work or hours of work. Another difference is whether the contractor performs work for other organisations or is entitled to do so. Other differences include whether the contractor has a separate place of work and advertises their services to the world at large; whether they pay their own income tax; whether they provide and maintain their own tools and equipment; and finally, whether the work can be delegated or subcontracted.

> **TIP:** Never provide any form of paid leave or ask an independent contractor to wear a company uniform.

A contract with an independent contractor can end in a number of ways:

- Because each party has fulfilled the obligations as per the contract,

- By agreement of both parties,

- By the operation of certain laws,

- By breach of the contract by one party, which then alters the other party's obligations as per the contract, or

- By 'frustration' of the contract due to unforeseen circumstances. This occurs when, through no fault of either party, the work entailed within the contract becomes incapable of being performed satisfactorily.

As an independent contractor, the individual has no recourse to legal remedies regarding dismissal; however, they do have some rights to general protections and provisions in the FWA. It is critical, therefore, that the lines between an employee and a contractor are made very distinct.

If there is a breach of contract, the affected party can choose either to treat the contract as still existing and hold the other party to their contracted commitments, or treat the contract as being terminated. If the contract is treated as terminated, the affected party can then seek the following remedies from a court:

1. Damages – These are likely to be the expected losses that the affected party would incur. The party affected must seek to minimise these costs. The principal finding an alternative contractor or the contractor trying to secure another contract as quickly as possible can achieve this.

2. Injunction – Stops a party from committing an act or carrying out a particular course of conduct.

3. Specific performance – Obtaining an order requiring a contractual party to perform its obligations as per the contract.

4. Declaration – A proclamation from a court for the purposes of resolving a conflict. This option is discretionary.

Labour-hire workers (otherwise referred to as temps)

This category covers those individuals who are supplied through a recruitment agency to work for a client company, generally for short periods of time. The agency may hire these individuals either as casuals or as independent contractors operating under a contract. The benefit for a business in this situation is that they are not the employer of the individual, and therefore are not responsible for the usual range of employee benefits. Instead, the agency is responsible.

Volunteers

Typically, volunteers are not employees. The reason for this is that, in order for there to be an employer-employee relationship, some form of 'consideration' is required, such as wages or a salary.

As volunteers are not deemed to be employees, they do not have the usual statutory rights that employees do regarding termination. However, they do have the right to a safe place of work as Workplace Health and Safety legislation covers all people in the workplace, including volunteers.

Which is right for you?

Each employment relationship carries different obligations and different rights for the employee. It is critical that you know and understand these differences and hire the correct type of worker for your needs.

WHAT TYPE OF EMPLOYEE WILL WORK BEST FOR ME?

Type of employee	Pros	Cons	Example situation
• Permanent full-time or part-time	• Both parties are committed to the longer-term relationship • Time to invest in long-term development of the individual • Stability for both parties • Costs are known	• Significant set up costs, in particular around Workers Compensation • Superannuation, Public Liability and Professional Indemnity need to be in place • You need to set up payroll and PAYG • More difficult to end employment if required	• Small business wins a significant piece of work with both tenure and margin built in • Business is growing and this warrants hiring an additional, say, customer service administrator
• Casual employees	• Short-term solution • Offers flexibility • You can find highly skilled casuals across a wide range of industries • You only need to give 24 hours' notice when there is no more work available • Can be employed from shift to shift	• You need to consider a rostering solution • If the work becomes regular, expected or lengthy the casual employee will be deemed to be a permanent employee • The casual can leave without notice	• Micro business experiencing significant and quick growth but unsure of the stability of the growth • Small café that, due to the closure of the restaurant next door, is experiencing an increase in customers

Type of employee	Pros	Cons	Example situation
• Independent contractors	• Great for project-type roles and tasks • You usually pay for the outcome rather than the time worked • All tools and equipment are supplied by the contractor	• You don't control how the work is done • The work can be subcontracted to a third party • Risk of being assessed as sham contracting • You still need to pay superannuation	• Small business needing to build a website and has no one in their network who can do this • A business is looking to move locations, which includes 300 employees across three locations. There is no one with this skill in-house, so a contractor is brought in to manage the project
• Labour-hire or temp	• Short-term solution • Externally payrolled • You are not the employer • You are able to exit the temp very quickly without repercussions • Longer-term assignments, such as nine months, are becoming more common	• Most suited to roles requiring generalist knowledge or skills such as reception or accounts payable • You are relying on the agency to be a good supplier of contingent workers	• Small business with an employee going on extended leave • Receptionist has a serious illness and is likely to need a couple of months of personal leave

Type of employee	Pros	Cons	Example situation
• Volunteer	• Family and friends are often happy to help out of love and the desire to see you be successful • Extremely cheap resource	• You still have a legal requirement to provide a safe place of work • You need to be very clear about both parties' expectations up front as these arrangements can sour very easily	• Start-up business run from home experiencing a peak in work around mail outs and answering phones • School canteens with mums and dads helping out with lunch orders

Now that you have determined how much work you have for an employee, where their role fits within your organisational plan and what types of employment are available, you will have a clearer picture of what will suit your business needs best. Next you need to become familiar with the legal framework around hiring employees and what your obligations are as an employer.

THE FOUNDATIONS – WHAT YOU NEED TO KNOW BEFORE HIRING ANYONE

Beyond knowing the type of employee you need and where they'll fit in your organisation, there are legislative items you need to be aware of before you hire anyone. Without being aware of the items covered under the Fair Work Act (FWA) and your relevant Modern Awards, you could easily breach one in your hiring, employment or dismissal of employees, with fines being $63,000 for corporations and $12,600 for individuals (per breach, remember!).

So, what are these legislative items? They include:

- Modern Awards that apply nationally for specific industries and occupations

- A set of ten minimum National Employment Standards (NES)

- Enterprise bargaining

- Protection from Unfair Dismissal

- Insurance (including Workers Compensation)

- Superannuation

These items are explained in more detail over the following pages.

Modern Awards

A Modern Award (also known as an Award) is a set of standards, including the minimum wages and conditions, to which an employee is entitled.

The first 122 Modern Awards commenced on 1 January 2010, coinciding with the introduction of the new national workplace relations system. We now have a total of 155 Awards recognised by Fair Work

Australia, which you can view at fwc.gov.au/awards-and-agreements/ awards/modern-awards/modern-awards-list

Do you know which Award your employees are covered under? Does it matter? The simple answer is yes, it does, and more than you might think.

Why? Well if you've hired before you'll remember the good old days when, as long as you paid above the Award, then none of the other requirements or clauses of the Award were applicable to you. *That is no longer the case.* Regardless of paying above the Award, all the other conditions of the Modern Award *must* be met unless there is a flexibility clause within that Award. Otherwise, you are in breach of the Award and breaches attract civil penalties.

So, what do you need to do?

Whether you are hiring your first employee or ensuring you are doing the right thing regarding your existing employees, follow these steps:

1. Identify the Award that covers your workplace: fairwork.gov.au/ awards-and-agreements/awards/find-my-award.

2. Check whether the terms and conditions of employment have changed.

3. Review and update employment contracts and policies to reflect the changes to terms and conditions (and incorporate the new terms and conditions into new contracts).

4. Consider appropriate Award classification levels – minimum wages, allowances, penalties and loadings.

5. Comply with non-monetary provisions of the Award, for example, consultation about major workplace change and dispute resolution.

6. Consider options to exempt high-income Award-covered employees, such as guaranteeing their annual earnings.

7. Consider how to transition existing employees to new rates of pay.

Initially, the Fair Work Ombudsman took a fairly relaxed approach to transitioning workplaces and subsequent breaches. However, given that Fair Work has now been in place for a number of years, if you are in breach, the full impact of the legislation could hit, including significant fines.

Keep in mind that the Modern Award minimum wages are reviewed annually by a panel put together from the Fair Work Commission. This comes into effect on 1 July of the following year, so ensure you stay informed to stay compliant – what might have been compliant last year might not be next year. You can review any changes at fairwork.gov.au/pay/minimum-wages/pay-guides and I would suggest that you make an annual diary note to check this in June each year.

Fair Work Australia National Employment Standards

Back in 2010 when FWA legislation came into play, so did the National Employment Standards, otherwise known as NES. These are nationwide standards and they cover the minimum employee conditions for all employees, including casual employees.

The national minimum wage and the NES make up the minimum entitlements for employees in Australia. An Award, employment contract, enterprise agreement or other registered agreement can't provide for conditions that are less than the national minimum wage or the NES. They can't exclude the NES.

All employees in the national workplace relations system are covered by the NES regardless of the Award, registered agreement or employment contract that applies.

So, what does this mean for you? Essentially there are ten minimum workplace entitlements in the NES, with which you must abide for all your employees.

1. **A maximum standard working week of thirty-eight hours for full-time employees, plus 'reasonable' additional hours.**

   It is important to have a conversation with the employee to help determine what is reasonable. In determining whether additional hours are reasonable or unreasonable, the following must be taken into account:

   - Any risk to employee health and safety
   - The employee's personal circumstances, including family responsibilities
   - The needs of the workplace or enterprise
   - Whether the employee is entitled to receive overtime payments, penalty rates or other compensation for (or a level of remuneration that reflects an expectation of) working additional hours
   - Any notice given by the employer to work the additional hours
   - Any notice given by the employee of his or her intention to refuse to work the additional hours
   - The usual patterns of work in the industry
   - The nature of the employee's role and the employee's level of responsibility
   - Whether the additional hours are in accordance with averaging provisions included in an award or agreement that is applicable to the employee, or an averaging arrangement agreed to by an employer and an award/agreement-free employee
   - Any other relevant matter

2. **A right to request flexible working arrangements to care for a child under school age, or a child (under eighteen) with a disability.**

   There are now more categories related to flexible working. I would stress having a conversation is part of making it reasonable rather than just rejecting outright.

What are flexible working arrangements?

Examples of flexible working arrangements include changes to:

- Hours of work (e.g. changes to start and finish times)
- Patterns of work (e.g. split shifts or job sharing)
- Locations of work (e.g. working from home)

Who can request flexible working arrangements?

Employees who have worked with the same employer for at least twelve months can request flexible working arrangements if they:

- Are the parent, or have responsibility for the care, of a child who is school aged or younger
- Are a carer (under the carer recognition act 2010)
- Have a disability
- Are fifty-five or older
- Are experiencing family or domestic violence, or
- Provide care or support to a member of their household or immediate family who requires care and support because of family or domestic violence.

Reasonable business grounds can include:

- The requested arrangements are too costly
- Other employees' working arrangements can't be changed to accommodate the request
- It's impractical to change other employees' working arrangements or hire new employees to accommodate the request
- The request would result in a significant loss of productivity or have a significant negative impact on customer service.

If a state or territory law provides an employee with a better entitlement to flexible working arrangements this will continue to apply.

3. **Parental and adoption leave of twelve months (unpaid), with a right to request an additional twelve months.**

This means potentially losing an employee for a period of two years – the upside is that if this is arranged up front it may be a more attractive option for a potential contractor who might be looking for some stability. Or you might look to bring someone into the role for career development on a temporary or secondment basis. From my experience to date, very few employees take the additional twelve months.

4. **Four weeks of paid annual leave each year (pro rata).**

There has been no real change here, but you may want to consider a forced shut-down – maybe at Christmas – to maximise productivity during more active periods of the calendar year. Check your Modern Award as there are timing and process issues to be considered. You can find your Award at: fairwork.gov.au/awards/how-to-find-an-award/pages/default

Employees accrue annual leave at 1.66 days per month. Part-time employees are entitled to leave on a pro rata basis, based on their proportion of ordinary hours worked. There is a provision for employees to be paid out their accrued annual leave entitlements on termination.

5. **Ten days of paid personal/carer's leave each year (pro rata), two days of paid compassionate leave for each permissible occasion and two days unpaid carer's leave for each permissible occasion.**

Personal leave covers sick leave but also leave to care for immediate family members as well. Employees can also take two days of compassionate leave and two additional unpaid days on each permissible occasion.

6. *Community services leave for jury service or activities dealing with certain emergencies or natural disasters. This leave is unpaid except for jury service.*

If you have employees who are members of the State Emergency Service (SES), Country Fire Authority (CFA) or similar, you need to have a contingency plan in place for when this employee might be on extended unpaid leave to cover their role and responsibilities. The other community service leave to take note of here is, should an employee be empanelled for jury service on a lengthy case, you will need to cover their role, but also continue to pay them.

7. *Long service leave.*

All states vary considerably regarding long service leave, so please refer to the relevant link in the *Resources* section.

8. *Public holidays and the entitlement to be paid for ordinary hours on those days.*

Some Awards will allow your employees to take a day in lieu for working a public holiday, but you will need to check your Modern Award(s) to ensure that you are able to do this. Here is a link to all Australian Public Holidays: australia.gov.au/topics/australian-facts-and-figures/public-holidays

9. *Notice of termination and redundancy pay.*

Before the introduction of the FWA 2010, you were only entitled to redundancy if it was a contractual clause, meaning that it was an entitlement of your employment. Now everyone is entitled, but their length of service only starts from 1 January 2010. So regardless of how much service you accumulated prior to this date, redundancy pay is only calculated from then, unless there was a previous entitlement under the contract of employment or a previous Award.

Please note that if you have fewer than fifteen employees, including casuals who are employed on a regular and systematic basis you can use the Fair Dismissal Code.

10. The right for new employees to receive the Fair Work Information Statement.

Employers must give every new employee a copy of the Fair Work Information Statement (the Statement) before, or as soon as possible after, they start their new job. (fairwork.gov.au/employment/fair-work-information-statement/pages/default.aspx)

Casual employees and the NES

Casual employees only get NES entitlements relating to:

- Unpaid carer's leave
- Unpaid compassionate leave
- Community service leave
- The Fair Work Information Statement

In some states and territories long serving casuals are eligible for long service leave. Where there is an expectation of ongoing work for a casual and the casual has been employed regularly and systematically for at least twelve months, they have extra entitlements from the NES.

These are:

- The right to request for flexible working arrangements
- Access to parental leave

Employees are becoming more aware of these rights. You need to be aware of your obligations and to determine if and how you can accommodate these types of requests, or whether you have the option to decline a request. As with all legislation, there are some processes that need to be followed. For example, the timeline for responding in writing to a request for flexible working is within twenty-one days of receipt. Make sure you and your management team are aware of these obligations. A good resource for this information is fairwork.gov.au

Enterprise bargaining

Enterprise bargaining is the term used to describe the event when employers and employees or their unions come together on a voluntary basis to negotiate the terms and conditions of employment. When agreement is reached this understanding is known as an enterprise agreement. Enterprise bargaining enables employers to negotiate out of some of the more onerous terms and conditions of the relevant Modern Award, however, the deal needs to satisfy the 'better off overall test' otherwise known as 'boot'. There is also likely to be a significant investment in time to work through all the options and, if you have a unionised workforce, it would include extensive negotiations with all relevant unions. An example of a benefit is often a higher rate of pay to offset the need to pay for overtime. As you would know the recording, management and payment of overtime can be a very involved process.

Protection from Unfair Dismissal

If you have fewer than fifteen employees, an employee that has under twelve months' service with you cannot make an Unfair Dismissal complaint against you. If you have fifteen or more employees, an employee must have six months of service before they can lodge an Unfair Dismissal complaint against you.

Insurance

Insurance is a little like death and taxes – you don't really want to go there but you probably will.

As the owner of a business, you face an ever-increasing number of potential exposures. Legislation is constantly changing, and the responsibilities associated with managing a business and having employees are complex and numerous.

When you are running your own business there are many insurances available, but you might not necessarily be aware of all of them or know which you need and how they relate to your particular exposure.

At a minimum, all businesses should have the insurances required by law, the insurances required by their Professional Associations and the insurances to protect them from other exposures such as the protection afforded by property insurance, directors and officers insurance, and so on.

Following is a list of the common types of insurances for businesses and business owners. Please keep in mind that you should discuss your individual circumstances with an insurer or insurance broker or intermediary to organise an appropriate level of insurance cover.

Workers Compensation insurance

Did you know that, from 2003 to 2016, 3,414 workers lost their lives in work-related incidents? That is, on average, twenty workers die per month at work. But this is just the tip of the iceberg, according to Safe Work Australia:

- A typical serious Workers Compensation claim involves five weeks' absence from work

- One quarter of serious claims require twelve or more weeks off work

- One in five serious claims involved a back injury

In 2015–16, the cause of serious claims was 90% due to injury and musculoskeletal disorders. Workers Compensation claims for disease accounting for the balance (the number of disease claims is likely to be underestimated, due to the difficulties associated with linking disease to workplace exposure). The most common injuries were traumatic joint/ligament and muscle/tendon injury (43%), and the interesting part is that these injuries can occur in both white-collar and blue-collar organisations.

Workers Compensation is a type of insurance that covers business's employees in the event of an injury or disease that occurs at work. The primary focuses of Workers Compensation are effective and early intervention of injury management and to create a safety net. The premise of the Act is to help facilitate an effective return to work.

Employers invest in Workers Compensation to insure themselves and cover their employees for compensation claims for workplace injuries.

Who needs it?

Workers Compensation is a statutory requirement – it is compulsory for all businesses that employ workers who are paid a wage (note some wage thresholds apply across jurisdictions), including family members, working directors and contractors. Independent contractors can be deemed workers if they are engaged on a systematic and regular basis. Workers Compensation may also be required for voluntary workers as well, depending on your jurisdiction requirements.

I recommend that you check your policy declaration requirements with your jurisdiction's insurer or regulator (see the *Resources* section of this book).

How is it priced?

In NSW, VIC, SA and QLD, premiums are underwritten and determined by the State. In ACT, TAS, NT and WA, insurers underwrite the business and set the price, with guidance from a Regulatory Gazette.

Premiums are generally calculated using the following:

[(Gross Wages x Industry Classification = Base Premium)
x Claims Experience*] + Legislative Levies

*Claims Experience is subject to Base Premium thresholds that serve to protect small business. E.g. In NSW, for Base Premiums under $30,000, the price of Workers Compensation is not impacted by Claims Experience. Where Claims Experience is applied, it usually considers the previous three to four years' claims history (frequency and cost), against the corresponding gross wages exposure and State and industry performance. In State-based schemes, the Claims Experience is calculated with a set formula. In jurisdictions underwritten by insurers, the insurer has more flexibility to price and will seek to understand the business's operating situation. This would include safety values, causes and nature of the claims in more depth. They may also complete assessments.

It is important to note that premiums are adjusted at the end of the insured period. This is because gross wages are estimated for the year to determine a price, claims for the coming year are unknown, and previous years claims costs change over time. Depending on how things change over the insured period, a business may get a refund premium, or may have to pay extra premium. So, I suggest you keep eye on any growth in gross wages or any escalating claims costs for your business as you may need to budget for increased premiums.

You can get Workers Compensation insurance by completing a proposal form with a broker, another intermediary or directly through an insurance company or Scheme Agent.

What are the benefits of having Workers Compensation?

Workers Compensation pays the following:

- Weekly payments in lieu of wages while an injured employee is unable to work. The major benefit here is that you no longer have to pay wages to somebody who is unable to work (it does not cover who is going to cover the absence, so you should do some contingency planning to prepare for this)

- Medical and hospital expenses

- Rehabilitation assistance, such as physiotherapists

- Lump sum payments for permanent impairment

- Treatment for certain diseases, if they are deemed to be work-related

Having the required insurance cover generates a more positive experience, even given the circumstances, that ensures an appropriate level of care and support. This should result in bringing the injured employees back to work as soon as possible, minimising the impact to productivity.

Where there is no insurance cover, the employee is left out of pocket until such time as a claim is recognised and accepted by the Nominal Insurer (State-based scheme that covers injured workers for non-insured employers). Exposing your workers to this can cause resentment and inhibits a safe return to work.

What are the risks/penalties if you don't have Workers Compensation cover?

If one of your employees lodges a claim, or your business comes under a random site inspection, which discovers you don't have a policy, there are heavy penalties. These may include fines and being charged an increased premium for the periods of non-insurance.

Further, in anticipation of workplace injuries to help expedite early intervention and speedy recovery, there are also regulatory obligations for larger employers to ensure that they have an injury management program and an employee with accountability for being the Return to Work Co-ordinator. The requirement to have a Return to Work Co-ordinator varies by jurisdiction, based either on number of employees or total wages.

Case study: Claim lodged against an uninsured employer

This case study is based on NSW Workers Compensation legislation.

Ms Citizen sustained an injury to her lower back on 10 May 2013 in the course of her employment. She was employed by the company and had been receiving wages since 2012.

A Workers Compensation claim was lodged against her employer following the workplace injury. However, the employer did not hold a Workers Compensation policy at the time of the injury. Therefore, the claim was lodged with the Nominal Insurer Scheme.

The nature of the injury resulted in Ms Citizen being totally incapacitated and unable to return to work. Her treatment plan included regular physiotherapy, pain management and a program of strengthening exercises at the gym. However, as there was no improvement in her condition, her medical specialist recommended surgery.

Ms Citizen received further medical treatment and participated in a rehabilitation program following surgery, resulting in her returning to work on restricted duties. Twelve months after being injured she was able to return to her pre-injury duties.

The full cost of Ms Citizen's claim (including weekly benefits, medical, rehabilitation and other costs) to the Scheme was $69,250.

Section 155 of the Workers Compensation Act 1987 (the Act), provides that all NSW employers must have (and maintain) a current Workers Compensation insurance policy. Furthermore, the legislation under section 156 of the Act provides that in the event of a non-insured period, the Authority may recover double the value of premium that should have been paid.

In calculating the relevant premium, the Authority audited the employer's financial records dating back five years (at a cost of $3,147.61) and found that the company had commenced operation from 1 July 2008 and had paid wages over five years totalling $527,104. The business had not held Workers Compensation insurance since it commenced.

The double-avoided premium of $20,209.17 was determined by multiplying the wages times the applicable Industry Classification (WIC) rates for each period of insurance. The applicable WIC rate was 1.917%.

As they were uninsured, the employer faced the following costs:

1. The full cost of the claim $69,250.00

2. Double-avoided premium in accordance section 156 $20,209.17

3. Cost of the wage audit   <u>$3,147.61</u>

                                       $92,606.78

The directors of the company could also potentially be fined $55,000 or spend six months in prison or both in accordance with Section 155 of the Act for not having a policy in place.

TIP: Familiarise yourself with your jurisdiction regulatory requirement for Workers Compensation.

Professional Indemnity insurance

As a business person running a company with a particular skill you are a specialist in your field. The law requires that you exercise the required skill at an appropriate level expected from such professionals. Your professional liability arises when there is a failure to provide this level of skill, which could negatively impact on a client (usually in a monetary sense).

Professional Indemnity insurance can assist with the damages awarded plus any costs or expenses incurred in defending the claim. As your business grows and you gain more employees, your risk will increase and it is important that you are sufficiently covered.

One very important point to remember about your Professional Indemnity Policy is that it is on a claims-made basis. This means that you must have a policy current when a claim is made irrespective of the date the failure occurred. Sometimes there can be a large gap in time between when the actual or alleged failure occurred and when the claim is first brought against you.

Also, it is crucial that your business activities are correctly described – if you have a Computer Programmer who sometimes provides Help Desk support as well, your policy must refer to *both* activities.

As with any insurance, this is always subject to the terms, conditions and exclusions contained in the actual policy. Some important exclusions are:

- Trade debts – the policy will not apply if you or your employees make an error that leaves you out of pocket; it is to cover your civil liability that leaves a client out of pocket
- Misquotes – if a quote is incorrect it will not be covered by the policy
- Insolvency of suppliers is not covered
- External fraud from third parties outside the company is not covered

Public Liability insurance

While Professional Indemnity insurance covers your liability for a breach of your professional duty (from the provision of advice), Public Liability insurance covers you for your legal liability for bodily injury or property damage to third parties, including customers.

These injuries may be a result of slips and falls, bumping someone accidentally, or accidentally damaging the property of others, and these can arise either at the business office, the business office contained within a residence, or away from the office while fulfilling the duties of your business.

As with Professional Indemnity insurance, as your employee numbers and need for space increase, so does your risk of accident to a third party and your need for Public Liability insurance.

Should you be unfortunate enough to cause one of these incidents and you do not possess adequate liability insurance you will need to mount your own defence, often a costly exercise. Should you lose; any damages awarded to third parties will need to be funded from your own resources which may involve the liquidating of assets, both business and private, if other resources are not available to you.

When you own a business, whether it be a shop front, home-based or an online business you do have exposures and you do need Public Liability insurance.

Public Liability insurance excludes the following:

- Any unlawful activity
- Any deliberate act to cause damage or injury
- Personal injury to you or your employees
- Property damage suffered by you or your employees

Business Insurance

Another insurance worth considering is Business Insurance, which is a combined policy that can cover a range of different risks in the one package, including fire and accidental damage for your contents and store/office fit-out, business interruption, burglary cover, money cover, glass cover, machinery breakdown, and electronic equipment breakdown. Sometimes Business Insurance may also include your Public Liability insurance.

Management Liability insurance

Every private company and its executives face an ever-increasing number of potential exposures, including:

- Employment Practices Liability, which covers discrimination, wrongful dismissal and/or sexual harassment of employees

- Theft of money by employees – over 10% of my clients have experienced this, and the amount totals over $1,000,000

- Breach of directors' duties, including breach of the Corporations Act

- Work Health and Safety breaches

- Investigations by regulators

- Breach of statutory duties

Management Liability insurance is a relatively new combination of Directors and Officers Liability, Employment Practices Liability and Fiduciary Liability insurance, which covers all of the above. Previously, this type of insurance was directed at large corporations and was not tailored to smaller private companies that faced many of the same exposures. However, given your increased awareness of your exposure, I would recommend that you seek advice about this level of protection.

Death and Disability insurance

Death and Disability insurance was particularly significant to me. I had been trying to get all my insurances in order before I started Employee Matters and, at the time, I was the main income earner. I had my medical and we were awaiting the confirmation it had been processed when separately, on my routine mammogram, they found a lump in my breast. I went through the 'oh sh*t' then 'what if I can't work – how are we going to support the family?' I was incredibly lucky the lump was benign, but what if it wasn't? What if I had gone through months of chemotherapy, too sick to work? I have had many friends go through cancer and the horrendous disease can be made even harder if you have additional financial worries.

Cybersecurity insurance

How fast time is passing, and our lives are changing – when I first released this book, Cybersecurity Insurance hardly existed. Now the Australian Government estimates that 700,000 businesses have experienced a cybercrime. 60% of these were targeted at small businesses with the average loss being more than $275,000. Costs are extensive and include the cost of Crisis Management, notifying your customers, IT system remediation and recreation of lost data and extortion costs.

Cyber insurance is now available from $300 per year and can provide protection for other exposures including system damage, business interruption, computer virus and hacking. Reduce your risk with regular backups (copies kept off site) and appropriate virus/security protection kept up to date.

Besides having in place quality Cyber and Privacy Protection Insurance, you need to ensure that your employees know what to watch out for. This includes unsolicited calls claiming to be from the bank, being very careful with customer details and who they are provided to, and clicking on unsolicited/dubious emails – one click is enough to activate a virus. All portable equipment should be password-protected/ encrypted to protect sensitive information.

Ensure you have protocols that are followed by all employees at all times. Should an attack happen, act immediately and contact your IT Provider. Be certain that you have a comprehensive Cyber and Privacy Protection Insurance Policy in place – if an attack happens, your broker will be able to put you in contact with specialist firms that can assist you through the incident.

Mandatory Breach Notification

On February 22, 2018 the Privacy Amendment (Notifiable Data Breaches) Act 2017 came into effect. The legislation requires Australian businesses that have been affected by a serious data breach to notify all customers whose information may have been compromised. If the organisation does not comply, heavy penalties may be imposed – fines of up to $420,000 for individuals and $2.1 million for organisations.

Currently the size of businesses impacted by this legislation concerns all organisations with turnover above $3 million, however if you are handling sensitive information, then this new legislation can still impact your business.

The OAIC advises that a data breach is eligible if it is likely to result in serious harm to any of the individuals to whom the information relates.

Three main areas for a notifiable data breach:

1. Unauthorised access to data – i.e. external attacker or employee browsing for no legitimate purpose

2. Unauthorised Disclosure – i.e. accidental publishing of a confidential data file

3. Loss – i.e. accidental loss of hard copies or unsecured computer equipment containing sensitive data – on public transport for instance.

Free Privacy Management Plan Template Here oaic.gov.au/resources/agencies-and-organisations/guides/privacy-management-plan-template.pdf

What will it cost you?

Insurance costs will vary greatly based on a large range of factors, such as:

- Occupation
- Turnover/fees
- Employee headcount
- Amount of coverage
- Sum insured
- Limit of indemnity required

The purpose of insurance is risk management – the part of the risk that can be transferred to someone else. It can prevent the ruin of your business and loss of your personal assets arising out of events that can and do happen.

It is always wise to review your insurance program. It is so easy for a business to start up, be told by someone – such as a landlord, an association or a supplier – that a certain type of insurance is required, and then everything is put away and forgotten. If your insurance hasn't been reviewed before, it should be looked at by your insurer or a broker who will provide recommendations on any gaps in your cover. You can then make the commercial decision on whether to accept the advice or not.

While penalties can arise from not having the statutory insurances (such as Workers Compensation), the real risk is being drawn into litigation that your business cannot pay for. In short, insurance is something that you always feel is a waste of money until you need to make a claim, and then you are so very glad that you have it.

> **TIP**: Should any circumstances arise that may result in a claim, you must immediately notify your insurer or insurance broker. Any delay in notification may result in your insurer refusing to accept your claim. It is also imperative that you do not admit liability.

Superannuation

Superannuation is a long-term savings structure used to save for retirement where money is put aside by an individual or the individual's employer and then invested in a range of options. These can be safe options such as cash, term-deposits and government-secured bonds, or more volatile options, such as Australian and overseas shares.

Most employers find setting up and contributing to superannuation time consuming and sometimes cumbersome, but there is no choice here – you must pay super to your employees and even yourself, depending on how you pay yourself from your business.

How much do you need to contribute to super?

The superannuation guarantee rate increased from 9.25% to 9.5% from 1 July 2014. The rate will remain at 9.5% until 30 June 2021, and then increase by 0.5 percentage points each year until it reaches 12% in 2025-26 as per the following:

2018–19 – 9.5%
2019–20 – 9.5%
2020–21 – 9.5%
2021–22 – 10%

2022–23 – 10.5%
2023–24 – 11%
2024–25 – 11.5%
2025–26 – 12%

(The above rate increases are based on laws as at September 2018.)

Penalties apply to employers who do not pay the required level of superannuation to their employees' nominated fund.

If employers do not meet their super obligations, they must lodge a quarterly Superannuation Guarantee Charge Statement (NAT 9599) and pay a superannuation guarantee charge. Additionally, your business might lose the tax deduction you would normally get for super contributions, because the super guarantee charge is not tax deductible, and neither are late super payments, if the late payment offset has been elected.

You will have to pay the super guarantee charge if you:

- Don't pay enough super contributions for your employees – this is called a super guarantee shortfall;

- Don't pay super contributions by the quarterly cut-off date for payment; or

- Don't pay super to your employees' chosen super funds – this is called a choice liability.

The super guarantee charge is made up of the super guarantee shortfall amounts (including any choice liability), nominal interest at 10% per annum, and an administration fee of $20 per employee, per quarter.

How often do I have to pay superannuation for my employees?

As an employer, you are required to pay the super guarantee percentage for your employees' gross wages at the end of each quarter as per the table below.

Quarter	Period	Payment cut-off date
1	1 July - 30 September	28 October
2	1 October - 31 December	28 January
3	1 January - 31 March	28 April
4	1 April - 30 June	28 July

Checklist – What I need before I hire

1. Have you determined that you need this employee? ☐

2. Have you confirmed that you can afford this employee? ☐

3. Have you got Workers Compensation insurance? ☐

4. Have you got Professional Indemnity insurance? ☐

5. Have you got Public Liability insurance? ☐

6. Do you know which Modern Award(s) your workplace (or this role) falls under? ☐

7. Have you decided what type of employee is most suitable for your business? ☐

8. Have you considered whether you could use a volunteer or casual employee? ☐

9. Have you drafted a job description? ☐

10. Have you got a legally compliant employment contract? ☐

11. Are you registered for PAYG Withholding? ☐

If you have checked off all these items, you are ready to begin the hiring process.

FINDING THE PERFECT MATCH

The groundwork has been laid – you know you need help and the type of help you need; you know which type of employees will best suit your requirements, and you know all the legislative items you need to take into consideration before any contracts get signed. Now it's time to start recruiting!

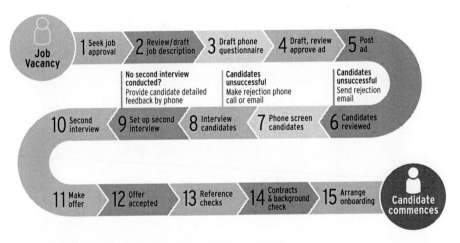

Step 1 – Determine your job vacancies

Any recruitment process starts with figuring out the jobs you need to fill. These will depend on your growth strategy and must fit within recruitment budgets. Refer back to the exercise in *Uh oh – I think I need some help!* to clarify what you need.

Step 2 – Recruitment approvals

While you may be the only one who needs to approve your first couple of hires, as you grow, recruitment approval forms can be used to help document approvals.

These forms need to be completed by the Hiring Manager (HM) and signed off by the Managing Director. The HM cannot commence recruitment until this form has been received. During this process, any internal candidates who may be suitable for the role need to be highlighted to the HM.

Step 3 – Prepare the job briefs

When preparing the job brief, you (or your HM) will need the following information:

- The knowledge, skills, abilities, and personal characteristics required to be successful in the role. These will help define the essential functions of the job,

- Ideal experience of the preferred candidate,

- Salary, bonuses and benefits aligned to the position,

- Ideal start date,

- Confirmation of the interview process,

- Outside-of-the-square factors – In a candidate-short market, it is sometimes impossible to get the ideal candidate. I would recommend compromising on the candidate's experience and industry background rather than competency requirements being reduced. Consider what this would look like – if you can attain 60% of what you are looking for in competencies and motivations, the 40% of experience or industry background can be improved through training,

- Hours of work, if not full-time permanent,

- Who the role will report to,

- Advertising strategy and budget aligned to the recruitment of the role,

- Employee value proposition (EVP) – why a candidate would want this role, and

- Any potential internal candidates who may apply for the role.

Step 4 – Advertising

Once you have an HM, they will write all advertising for new roles, which must be reviewed and approved prior to posting the ad externally. To advertise, use Seek, Standout ads, all free job boards, the careers page on your website and your company LinkedIn page, if you have one.

You can now also advertise roles on LinkedIn and Facebook, which can be very effective at targeting people in the enormous databases who are a match for your role, particularly in LinkedIn. Although, LinkedIn has recently changed their pricing structure to a 'pay per click' one, it is still a good source for candidates.

Step 5 – Candidate communication

Once you have an HM, they will assess all applications against the job brief.

Emails should be sent to all unsuccessful candidates within two working days of receiving their application.

Depending on the number of successful applications, you may choose to assess them with a phone screen, which will be tailored to match the job brief. All unsuccessful candidates following the phone screen should receive an email advising them, within two working days.

Questions that you might ask could be:

1. What attracted you to this opportunity?
2. Tell me about your experience that is relevant to this role.
3. Can you give me a brief overview of your background?
4. What are your primary skills?
5. How would your team members describe you?
6. What are your salary expectations?

7. When would you be available to start?

8. Do you have a right-to-work visa? If yes, which one?

Completing a preliminary phone screen should either confirm your interest in proceeding to a face-to-face interview or give you additional data to move to a decision to reject at this stage of the process. It will give you a sense of the candidate's phone manner and communication skills, at a minimum.

Successful phone screen candidates should be provided with information about your recruitment process, including reference and background checking requirements. Ideally, the first reference check should be conducted in preparation for the next interview.

Step 6 – Interviews

I believe that a lack of interview skills is one of the key reasons that employers select the wrong candidate and, as a result, end up with an employee who either does not have the skills to do the job or is the wrong cultural fit. This problem is usually due to most entrepreneurs not being formally taught how to interview. I'm sure you can relate – if you were lucky, you might have been able to sit in on an interview with your manager before leaving the corporate world. That's okay if the interviewer was sophisticated and technically strong, but horrendous if the interviewer was poor.

If there is one skill that I would encourage you to work on, it is your interview technique. Not only will this skill help you hire the right employees, it will also assist you with general communication skills such as active listening and probing, as well as performance management interviews or investigations.

Organising the interviews

As a part of your recruitment process, ensure your administrator confirms the availability of the HM so that interviews can be set up promptly with the candidates. Your HM will need to be as flexible as possible with their time, as candidates may have work commitments they need to juggle.

Once an interview is organised, confirm the details by email.

Preparing for interviews

Your interview preparation will enable you to select the best candidate for the role, as well as present yourself and your business in a professional manner to encourage the candidate to really want to work for your organisation.

Use the following as a checklist when preparing for your interview:

- Ensure that you have booked an office or somewhere you will be able to talk privately. Ideally not at the local coffee shop, as this can be distracting and make the candidate very self-conscious.

- Confirm the name of the interviewee and the expected time with your team so they can be welcomed appropriately.

- Ensure that you have read their application and CV in detail and that you have prepared your questions in advance (refer to the *Resources* section for sample questions).

- Make certain that there will be no interruptions and that your mobile is switched off. The candidate should have your undivided attention. (I would hope that the candidate has also turned their phone off.)

During the interview

An interview should be one hour long and well-documented. Regarding the time allowed, remember that some candidates may be interviewing in their lunch break. The last thing you want to have happen is that the candidate is distracted and trying to look discreetly at their watch while simultaneously answering your questions and thinking of a believable excuse as to why they are late back to work. This scenario is not at all conducive to putting their best interview performance on show.

If possible, organise for two employees to be present in interviews so that you can share thoughts and notes afterwards (ideally the HM and someone from the team the candidate will be joining, if not the manager of that team).

Finally, all successful candidates should be interviewed at least twice. It is also good practice to have the candidates meet with other team members prior to any offers being made.

Introduction (5–10mins)

Start by walking to your reception area and warmly greeting the candidate with a firm handshake and a smile. (Don't forget the smile – first impressions count.)

As you walk to the interview room, build rapport with small talk – 'Did you find us okay? Isn't it hot today?' This will start to put the candidate at ease (remember, they are likely to be somewhat nervous and you want them to be relaxed and willing to talk and share with you). Also make sure that they are comfortable; have them remove their coat and ask them if they would like some water. (Better still, assume this and have it ready for them.)

Begin the interview by introducing yourself and explaining the process, 'Thank you for coming to speak with me today. My name is Jessica Brown and I am the Operations Manager. I would like to talk with you in detail about some of the experiences that you have had in the past and what you are looking for in your next role. Towards the end of the interview I will share with you some more detail about the role and what skills we are looking for and more information about our business. You will then have a chance to ask me some questions if you like. The interview usually takes about an hour – is this time okay with you?'

Before you start asking questions, tell the candidate that you may interrupt them now and then to ensure that they stay on track and you can cover all the details required. Tell them that you will be taking detailed notes so that you can remember all the great things they say. This puts candidates at ease and deters the urge to try and read what you are writing upside down.

Finally, before you launch into the main body of the interview, ask them if they have any questions before you start.

Body of interview (40–50mins)

The body of the interview is all about asking questions and listening. Remember to only talk for 20% of the time – *the candidate should be speaking for the other 80% of the interview.* This can be very difficult for some interviewers, but it is the only way that you can effectively tease out all the information you require.

Ask your prepared questions (see the *Resources* section for a list of sample interview questions); a combination of technical, behavioural and cultural aspects. Choose six to ten behavioural questions that are relevant to the circumstances the candidate may experience if they were successful and joined your business.

Use active listening techniques – this means eye contact, 'ah, ahs' and maybe 'can I just check my understanding? So, what I think you were saying was that...'

Remember to probe. Don't allow a candidate to skim over answers; continue to dig until you have the information that you require or until you are satisfied that you understand the scenario that they were talking you through. Also, don't be afraid to interrupt to keep the interview on track and to gather the information that you are seeking.

Look for the emotions behind their words and look at their body language (and your own) to ensure that it is appropriate. Remember, 65% of communication occurs through body language.

Summarise occasionally for the interviewee to show them that you are listening. It's also another way of practising active listening. Candidates love it – give it a go. Everyone wants to be heard.

Finally, take detailed notes. It's okay to pause and catch up on your note taking. I usually say something like, 'That was great, let me just check that I have captured everything correctly'.

TIP: Do not, *under any circumstances*, lean back in your chair and put your arms behind your head.

Closing the interview (5–10mins)

Explain the role in more detail, ensuring that you portray the role and the opportunities realistically. Do not overstate the role, otherwise this could lead to an early resignation due to the role not meeting the expectations set during the recruitment process. However, do sell the benefits of working for your business, why it is a great place to work and what you like about it.

Explain your background and role and highlight what you have done in your time with the business.

Ask them if they have any questions. They should, and they might be questions such as:

- Why do you like to work here?
- What date would the new hire be expected to start?
- Your website says that one of your values is integrity; can you please give me an example of when you have seen this value in action?
- What are the goals for the business over the next eighteen months?
- Where do you see the opportunities for this individual in eighteen months' time?
- Do you support related external study financially?

Explain what will happen next, along the lines of 'Well thank you Jenny, it has been lovely to meet you today. We are interviewing a number of candidates this week and we expect to have a shortlist of individuals to interview for a second time by Monday, with offers by the end of the week. Does this timing work for you?' (You want to establish whether there are any competing offers in play at the moment.)

Finally, stand up and escort them to the door or lift, thank them again for their time and shake their hand and smile.

After the interview

Now it's time to return to the office and write your assessment of the candidate. Do not leave the room until this is completed; if you do, you will forget some details and not assess the candidate as effectively or fairly as you could have when it was all fresh in your mind. To make comparisons easier and more accurate, ensure you ask all candidates the same questions.

While sometimes difficult, it is imperative that you do not make any assessments or judgements based on race, colour, gender, religion, political opinions, national extraction, social origin, age, medical record, criminal record, marital status, physical disability, sexual preference, intellectual or psychiatric disability or trade union activity.

Candidates who are unsuccessful after the interview should be provided detailed feedback by phone. Only email if you can't contact the candidate. All notes on the conversation should be placed on the file.

Successful candidates (either those who progress to a second interview or those you want to offer a position) should then have their references checked.

Step 7 – Identity, reference, background and visa checks

When you hire employees there is a high level of trust required on both sides. From your side, for example, you may want to know that your employee will treat your company equipment appropriately and handle cash in a trustworthy manner. From the employee side, they want to know that the role that you are offering is as you said it would be and that you will take your duty-of-care obligations seriously. Your duty-of-care obligations are the legislative obligations you have as an employer, such as ensuring the workplace and work practices are safe. High levels of trust lead to high levels of engagement.

That said, you might be surprised to discover that identity theft is on the increase in Australia. According to the Australian Bureau of Statistics Personal Fraud Survey 2014–15, Australians lost $3 billion due to personal fraud. More alarmingly, the survey estimated a total of 1.6 million Australians aged fifteen years and over were victim of at least one incident of card fraud in the twelve months prior to the survey.

Did you know that the most common acts of fraud, according to research from KPMG, are the theft of cash, false invoicing and diversions of sales? The cost of fraud is considered to be around $345 million with respondents believing that *only a third* of the total losses are being detected. It is a very real problem and one that can be reduced by background checking, internal controls and by not ignoring red flags.

Additionally, did you know that research estimates that over 35% of candidates lie about their skills and experience on their resumes and at interview? These lies can be about a six-month holiday by the sea that was actually a stint in jail, or a resignation that was actually a termination for fraud.

Finally, did you know that if you inadvertently hire an employee whose right-to-work visa has expired, you can be exposed to significant fines? The Department of Home Affairs defines an illegal worker as a non-citizen who is working without a valid visa, or working in breach of a visa condition. It is worth noting that not everyone who comes to Australia on a visa has permission to work.

The onus is on you to check their visa status, so it needs to form part of your recruitment process. We recommend that you have every candidate bring their passport to the interview. This passport will not only enable you to check their right-to-work status but will also provide identity confirmation.

As you can see there are a variety of fines, so the main take away message is to check every candidate's and employee's right to work. Also, many visas have an expiry date, so also make sure that you have set up a calendar entry to check visas prior to expiry and to confirm that an extension has been approved or permanent residency has been granted.

	Maximum penalty
Illegal Worker Warning Notice	Administrative warning
Infringement	$3,780 fine for individuals $18,900 fine for bodies corporate
Civil penalty	$18,900 fine for individuals $94,500 fine for bodies corporate
Criminal offence	$25,200 fine and/or two years imprisonment for individuals $126,000 fine for bodies corporate
Aggravated criminal offence	$63,000 fine and/or five years imprisonment for individuals $315,000 fine for bodies corporate

How can you protect yourself from employees who might fall into the above categories? Just add a little rigour to your process.

Identity checks

Whenever you are interviewing for a role, ask the candidate to bring along their passport, driver's licence or other suitable form of ID to the interview. The passport will assist you both with the ID check and their right-to-work status. Most candidates will not have a problem with this request. Check the passport and take a photocopy for your records. This way you know that the candidate is who they say they are. If the individual is reluctant to provide this evidence, I would be concerned as to why.

Reference checks

I know that a lot of business owners don't see any value in reference checks, assuming that candidates will just share the referees that they know are going to give them a good reference, but I disagree. You should complete at least two references per candidate and they should be completed with the individual who was their direct supervisor in their previous two roles. Ideally the first reference check should be conducted prior to interview and the second reference check should be taken post interview, if you are looking to move to an offer.

Referees should be individuals the candidate has reported to directly in the last three years. A trick is, when discussing the current and previous role, to ask who or what position they reported to. This can be checked later with a call to the receptionist.

I believe that reference checks provide another data point that you may not have gleaned in the interview about strengths and areas for development from a manager's perspective. I also believe that with a reference check it is not so much what the referee says but what they don't say.

A word of caution – they may endeavour to steer clear of slander territory. They might believe that it is better to just confirm the role and the candidate's length of service. Ideally, the individual conducting the reference check should then ask the follow-up question, 'Is that your company policy: to only provide title and tenure?' If they answer 'No', then proceed with caution. You must also consider that there may have been a personality conflict with a particular referee, and, if you are really keen on the applicant, consider a third reference check to get a balanced view.

Background checks

Depending on the role, I believe that it is very much worth the investment of completing background checks, especially if the role is one that handles large amounts of cash! Background checks are typically completed by a third party and can consist of the following:

- Police checks
- Credit checks
- Education history
- Working with Children checks

As you can imagine, with more and more candidates coming from overseas, it can be even more important to check facts, but be aware that this takes time.

Candidates should be made aware that if anything arises from the background checks that is a concern their employment offer can be rescinded at any time.

When I was working in India we had hired 500 people in five weeks, a massive undertaking and not without its challenges. It was discovered that a number of hires had submitted fake degrees for qualifications that they did not have or that they had inflated marks. The interesting point to note was that a number of these employees were performing to expectation, but the reality was that they had deliberately lied and misled the organisation. One of this organisation's core values was integrity, so on this basis the outcome was that all employees involved were terminated.

Any concerns that are raised must be kept confidential due to the Privacy Act. Only with the permission of the candidate can any information be shared with other individuals within the business.

Visa checking

An often-misunderstood obligation of employers is that they are responsible for checking the right-to-work status for all employees working for them. As an employer, you are liable for any individuals working illegally for your business. Upon hiring, the best way to check is to review the passport for the relevant visa and the end date, and to take a copy of this. Ideally this should have been completed at the interview stage, but if it hasn't this needs to happen as part of induction. An even better way is to use a government website called VEVO (Visa Entitlement Verification Online). homeaffairs.gov.au/busi/visas-and-migration/visa-entitlement-verification-online-(vevo)#tab-content-1

Once you have set up an account as an employer organisation, it is as simple as popping in the individual's passport number and *voila* – details are made available. Then I recommend you diarise to check this quarterly in case the visa is cancelled for any reason that is not revealed to you by the employee.

Should you have employees on visas with expiration dates, ensure you note these and regularly review the visa status with the employee.

In all employment contracts, I would recommend that you have a clause that states, 'Should any outstanding reference or background checks come back negatively, we reserve the right to terminate the contract.' These checks can save you significant time and money so are worth the effort.

Why might a small business consider sponsoring an employee's visa?

The main reason you might want to consider sponsoring an employee's visa is that there might be a shortage of a very specific skill set within your company that you are unable to source locally. The skills may be vital to the success, growth or even the continuation of your business.

Often these skills can be found in a candidate from overseas and this person can then teach these skills to your existing employees. Alternately, the business may have employed someone on a working holiday visa where they may work full-time for the company for six months and may wish to sponsor them on expiry of their visa, owing to the benefits they are bringing to the business.

Another benefit is that you could increase the suite of products your business is able to offer by taking on someone with a new skill. Also, by taking on someone with another language, your business could potentially start operating internationally.

What are the risks and what do I need consider when making the decision to sponsor?

As a sponsor, you must fulfil the sponsorship obligations and these obligations include simply paying the visa holder to the level of the minimum threshold set out in their employment contract. The sponsorship obligations are a list of requirements the company must abide by, which also include reporting any changes of the company address or status to Department of Home Affairs (DHA), and reporting within twenty-eight days that a sponsored employee has left the business. If these obligations are not met, then you risk losing your sponsorship status. For further information on the obligations please refer to: homeaffairs.gov.au/trav/work/work/temporary-residence-sponsor-obligations

What types of visa are available to small businesses?

There are three main types of visas available to small businesses – the Temporary Skills Shortage (482) visa, the Employer Nomination Scheme and a Training Visa (407).

The **TSS (482)** is the most common – this is a visa originally designed to temporarily fill skill shortages within the Australian workforce with the idea that, in the meantime, Australians themselves could up-skill and train to take over these positions in the future.

The **186 Employer Nomination Scheme** was designed to allow employers to nominate an overseas employee for a permanent residence visa. This will be either after three years on the 482 Visa (or two years if the applicant held or applied for a 457 visa prior to April 19th, 2017) with that business, or by the 186 Direct Entry Stream.

The 186 Direct entry stream is where the visa applicant can qualify for immediate permanent residence by proving their skills with a Skills Assessment (recognition of overseas qualifications by the appropriate assessment authority in Australia), demonstrating at least three years of full-time work in the nominated occupation, and obtaining the desired English language level.

The **Training Visa (407)** is a little-known visa that allows you to employ an overseas worker, up-skill them and then promote them to a higher-level position than they commenced in. It allows you to pay them an Award wage for the position, rather than a wage dictated by the TSS 482 visa. Due care must be taken with this visa application, which involves providing a detailed training plan and ensuring that the person does actually require the training and does not already hold the skill set to perform the role. Otherwise, the DHA will suspect that the small business is trying to get out of paying the market rate for the TSS 482 visa.

The transition from the 457 to 482 TSS visa

2017 and 2018 brought significant change to the visa landscape in Australia. The Department of Home Affairs has sought to tighten the requirements for both temporary and permanent visa schemes and this has resulted in a lower intake of visa applicants across the different visa subclasses. The biggest change has been to the occupation lists that are available to be used for a permanent residency visa application. Previously over 600 occupations were able to be used to progress from a temporary 457 visa to a 186 visa by way of the temporary residency transition stream (working for two years for the one employer).

Since July 2017, a split list of more than 450 occupations is available for a 482 Temporary Skill Shortage (TSS) visa (previously 457) with only approximately 200 occupations now allowing the applicant to progress to a 186 permanent residency application. This Medium to Long-term Strategic Skills List (MLTSSL) is dominated by Medical, Information Technology, Trades, Accounting and Health Care professions that generally require a degree or trade qualification.

The remaining 250+ occupations on the Short-term Skilled Occupation List no longer afford the visa applicant the opportunity to progress to a 186 permanent residency visa application. Occupations on this list generally do not require a degree or trade qualification.

These changes are designed to meet the skills requirements of the nation going forward, to assist Australians in having access to all jobs available and, last but not least, to discourage HR Directors and Professionals from using the 482 visa subclass as part of their hiring and Talent Management strategies.

This change in legislation has had significant impact on businesses that have hired skilled individuals with occupations on the Short-term Skilled Occupations List in the past. Regardless of the views and opinions of this change in legislation, HR Professionals and Directors must now reconsider their hiring strategies and you must consider the impact on applicants who may not be able to build tenure and stay in Australia permanently.

So why should you continue to access the 482 subclass visa scheme?

Let's talk about what has changed for the better. In the past, businesses have had to prove that they were spending equal to 1% of their payroll on the training of Australian workers. For those employers with a large payroll, this created a difficult benchmark to reach and discouraged some potential sponsors.

As of the 12th August 2018, Sponsors no longer have an obligation to provide this 1% proof of training as the Department of Home Affairs has replaced this with a simple Skilling Australia Fund Levy. This levy changes given the level of business' turnover, and businesses with turnover of less than $1 million per annum are charged $1,200 per year of the visa offered to the applicant.

Why is that good? Simply, the cost of compliance with the previous benchmark was onerous on businesses and the new levy is simple and payable. The barriers to becoming a sponsor are therefore lower for some employers.

Another change is that all 482 Visa Applicants must show proof of two years of relevant experience in the occupation being applied for in the 482 application. This is a change from the previous scheme where discretion was given to inexperienced applicants.

The rules concerning the advertising of the visa applicant's position have also been tightened as of the 12th of August 2018. Now sponsors (or their recruitment agents) must run the advertisements for the role in question for thirty days, quoting the annual salary (or salary range). Where advertisements were paid for, the sponsor must prove receipts of payment for this advertising.

With changes to possible permanent residency, experience of the visa applicant (which most already had) and a tightening of advertising and a transparent training levy, why should the HR community be less inclined to access the 482 visa scheme? Well there is no impediment to that, but the key question becomes:

'How do I manage the change in tenure among my visa-holding employees?'

Let's look at a scenario. Chris is a recruitment consultant (an occupation on the Short Skills list) and he has just had his visa granted. He is as happy to be working for his Australian employer and he sees a medium-term future in Australia. Chris has been informed that he will be able to renew his two-year 482 visa at the two-year mark and obtain a further two years of visa tenure. At a date four years after the initial visa grant date, Chris will need to leave Australia.

The key question is: how do businesses manage the fact that Chris will not be able to continue in the business after those four years, and what will be the effect on the company culture as Chris works into his last year knowing he has to depart?

This scenario will take time to manifest itself in the Australian business landscape; however, it will be a relevant issue come 2020 – 2022 as the first 482 visa holders come to an end of their two- to four-year tenure.

What is involved in sponsoring someone for a TSS 482 visa?

Getting a TSS visa involves three steps:

1. **Sponsorship**

   You must show financial records to prove your business has the ability to sponsor the visa applicant. This includes showing proof of sufficient turnover to facilitate the wages required to pay a TSS 482 Visa applicant. The business must also show they are currently employing Australians by submitting organisational charts and other evidence.

2. **Nomination**

   In this stage you nominate a specific position for the TSS 482 applicant, which must meet the following requirements:

   • The position must be demonstrated to be genuine, so an organisational chart is required along with genuine temporary entry statements.

   • The market salary for the position must be paid above the minimum of $53,900 plus super per annum, meaning the same wage as an Australian would earn employed in the same position.

- The occupation must appear on the Department of Home Affairs' MLTSSL or SSTOL Occupations List. An occupation on the MLTSSL will provide for a visa of up to four years in length. An Occupation on the SSTOL list will enable a two-year visa to be granted.

- Advertising must be submitted to show genuine efforts by employers to have tested the Australian market prior to submitting a nomination for the visa applicant. The advertising must run for thirty days on national online, print or broadcast media. Employers (or their Agents) must show proof of payment for such ads.

3. **TSS 482 Visa**

   Finally, the applicant must meet the visa requirements:

- The applicant must demonstrate two years of work experience in the skill set required to perform the duties of the nominated occupation; and

- The applicant must have an IELTS (International English Language Testing System) of 4.5 for each band for SSTOL occupations and 5.0 for MLTSSL occupations, unless from an exempt country, such as the UK, Canada, or the USA.

What if I want to nominate an overseas employee for permanent residency?

If you have an employee who has been on the 457 visa for two years or a TSS 482 Visa for three years, you may want to apply for a permanent residency visa through the Employer Nomination Scheme (ENS).

What are the costs?

The costs of sponsoring an overseas employee vary according to whether or not professional assistance is sought. At the time of writing, these stand at $420 for the sponsorship application, $340 for the nomination, and $1,175 for each visa applicant who applies for a position on the SSTOL list or $2,455 for an applicant who applies for an occupation on the MLTSSL. If more than one person is coming to Australia on the same visa (such as a spouse), you will need to pay for those applicants as well.

If the visa applicant is applying for second visa onshore (so the applicant has already received one temporary visa while being onshore in Australia), there is an additional subsequent onshore fee payable of $700.

Many visa applicants move to Australia when their visa is approved and have their spouse and family join them within six to twelve months after they have settled into the job and their new surrounds. This is not a complex process, but in some cultures, bringing your partner can create an issue of choice. Our Migration Agent shared the following story with us:

'When interviewing an applicant in Southern Africa in 2007, my business partner and I were concluding an interview with a prospective Diesel Mechanic who had met all our criteria for the visa when we mentioned to him that he could bring his wife. At this point he looked strained and puzzled and we could not work out why. Did this evoke memories of a wife deceased; did his wife not want to come; had he been left jilted at the altar?

He paused for a moment and said, "Ah but I have four wives. Can I bring all four to Australia?"

As we explained to him that only one wife could be identified to join him on his visa he, without so much as a blink of an eye, stated,

"Okay, I will bring the youngest one".

Dealing with different cultures is, of course, interesting. But it's also important when understanding their thinking and explaining the limitations of the Visa legislation.'

Costs to have this whole TSS 482 process undertaken by a migration professional, which I highly recommend for this complex application, may vary from approximately $4,000 to $8,000. This depends upon the level of complexity of the case, and whether or not the company has a sponsorship agreement already in place.

How do I check someone's visa status?

The easiest way to do this is via VEVO (homeaffairs.gov.au/busi/visas-and-migration/visa-entitlement-verification-online-(vevo)), which allows you to directly input the applicant's passport details and ascertain whether or not work rights have been granted as a condition of the visa. If you either accidentally or intentionally employ someone who cannot lawfully work, or an employee works more hours than they are legally entitled to, it can result in fines of over $30,000. It may also make it almost impossible for you to sponsor anyone in the future, should the need arise.

On-Hire Labour Agreements

An On-Hire Labour agreement allows a business to sponsor an applicant through a third party, (an On-Hire Labour agreement holder).

The best way to think about this model is if you do not want to employ employees, then you can put them on as contractors, employed by a recruiter or employee management company. The On-Hire Labour agreement model is similar – it allows an applicant to be sponsored by a third party so the host employer does not need to be concerned with the sponsorship obligations mentioned earlier. The On-Hire Labour agreement provider charges a margin per month in the same way that a recruiter would charge a margin per month on a contractor.

Who can help me do this?

The best advice is to speak with a Registered Migration Agent. You can find a Registered Migration Agent on the website of the Office of the Migration Agents Registration Authority (mara.gov.au).

The changes made by the Department of Home Affairs in the past twelve to eighteen months have made applying for any visa extremely complex and not a task for any business person. It is even harder to resolve if a mistake has already been made with a lodged application. It's much better to seek advice in advance of lodgement from an experienced Registered Migration Consultancy who is well versed in the current legislation in immigration law. (I have recommended one in the *Resources* section.)

How should I look to manage this on an ongoing basis in my business?

To manage this on an ongoing basis, it is best to enter into a relationship with a professional migration consultancy and seek advice regularly, on all the aspects of employer sponsorship that apply to your business.

This way, if the Department of Home Affairs do later decide to conduct an audit of your business, you will have an experienced professional to assist you in providing the correct information and avoiding any undue headaches or sleepless nights.

> **TIP**: Do not do this by yourself. Self-managed migration case lodgement can end disastrously for both the company and the visa applicant. It may look like a simple online application, but there is much to consider in preparing a decision-ready application that can be approved immediately by the Department of Home Affairs.

MAKING THE OFFER – HOW TO GET THEM TO SAY 'I DO'

When you've found the right candidate for the job, your Hiring Manager (HM) should make a verbal offer of employment, which is then confirmed by email prior to the formal paperwork being sent out. The candidate's acceptance needs to be confirmed before the letter of offer and contract of employment can be drawn up.

And, should the candidate not accept the role, this is a valuable opportunity to get feedback. Consider asking some or all of the following questions:

- May I ask why you have rejected our offer?

- Was the other role paying more compensation? If so, how much?

- What attracted you to the other role?

- How did you find our recruitment process?

- Is there anything that we could have done differently that would have changed your decision?

To close, invite the candidate to contact you again if the other role doesn't work out for them, wish them every success and thank them for considering your company. After speaking to the candidate, ensure detailed feedback is provided to the HM.

The letter of offer

The letter of offer confirms the verbal offer and acceptance and is sent with two copies of the employment contract. A basic template might look like the following:

Sample offer letter

Company letterhead
Date
Applicant name
Applicant address

Dear applicant name,

Thank you for your interest in ABC. As per our discussion, we would like to extend an offer to you for the role of *position title* commencing on *date.*

Please find attached our employment contract for your review and consideration. Please indicate your acceptance of this offer of employment by signing both copies and returning one copy to us by *date.* Should we not receive acceptance by this date, this offer will lapse.

Should you have any questions regarding the documents please contact me on *your work phone number* to discuss.
We very much look forward to you joining ABC.

Yours sincerely,

Name
Position

The employment contract

To have a contract or not to have a contract – that is the question! With small businesses that are growing quickly, it is very common for an employment contract to be hastily pulled together to bring on new employees.

To get a contract quickly, many business owners borrow (or crib from) a mate's employment contract. What often happens then is that various managers amend them (often unbeknownst to the owner) and they end up with numerous versions, ranging from ones that aren't legally binding to, in some instances, having no contract whatsoever.

But if you only hire trustworthy people, that isn't a problem. Or is it?

Here are the top five reasons why you need to get your employment contracts in order:

1. **Sets the scene** – When someone is considering joining your organisation, one of the first impressions that they receive is the employment contract. This sets the tone for what they can expect life to be like as an employee of your company and what is important to your business. Having a clear, professional and legally binding contract can assist you in attracting the right kind of employee.

2. **Consistency** – Imagine if Jeff in accounts has negotiated into his contract an additional week of paid annual leave; first, this is a costly concession that has been agreed to and second, you immediately have an equity issue – do you reduce Jeff's allowance back to four weeks or up everyone else's leave to five weeks? It is important to ensure that everyone is treated the same way, especially as you grow, otherwise you can get bogged down in employee warfare. (There may be some instances when this inequity can be justified however – maybe Jeff has been there five years longer than everyone else.)

3. **Not compliant with Fair Work Act changes** – The FWA came into effect 1 January 2010 and with it came a number of minimum standards to which all employees across Australia are entitled. You need to ensure that the employment contract is compliant with the FWA, the NES and the relevant Modern Award(s). Do you know what these are? If not, you are potentially in breach of the FWA and you should correct this immediately. Go back to *The foundations – what you need to know before you hire anyone* to get started.

4. **Uncertainty of rights and expectations** – To save confusion, everyone should be very clear about their rights – both employer and employees. This generally reduces potential conflicts.

5. **What happens when someone leaves?** – It is a business reality that people will leave your organisation and, when they do, you need to be protected against them taking client information, intellectual property and other employees with them. Unless this is in the contract, it is poor form but perfectly legal.

What to include in an offer of employment

Beyond the legal bases you need to cover with your employment contract, there are certain items that will be candidate-specific. After you've selected a candidate, the Hiring Manager should provide all offer details so that the employment contract can be drawn up. These include:

- Title of the role
- Base salary plus super
- Any incentive or bonus structure aligned to the role
- Start date
- Probation period
- Standard working hours
- Who the role is reporting to and the title of that role

When making an offer of employment, the Fair Work Information Statement must be sent out to all permanent employees with their employment contract and letter of offer. You can find it at: fairwork.gov. au/employment/fair-work-information-statement/pages/default.aspx

Finally, I would recommend that you regularly review and potentially amend your employment contract and related documentation every two to three years, especially if there are legislation changes.

Remember, the employment contract and documentation set the framework for the way that you employ people and it protects your business in the long term. It shows that your employees matter to you, so take the time to do it well!

PART 2: MANAGE

FROM GOOD TO GREAT – ORGANISATIONAL DEVELOPMENT

We started *Part 1: Hire* by looking at organisational planning to ensure that you hired the right people to allow your business to grow the way you wanted. What might surprise you is that you can't just leave the organisation chart and job descriptions you created once you've hired everyone – your business and your team are going to evolve over time, and your organisational structure and the roles within it will need to develop to support that evolution.

To ensure your organisation continues to develop well, we're going to revisit your organisation chart, your job descriptions and your transition plan.

Phase 1 – Organisation charts

1. Review your existing organisation chart. Who sits where, who reports to whom and what are their titles and levels of responsibility? Is it up to date, or do you only have your original chart to refer to? If you only have your original chart, sketch out your current one.

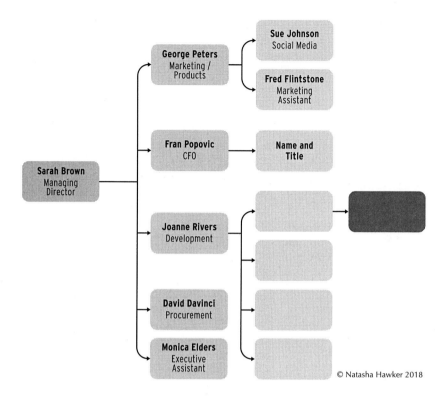

© Natasha Hawker 2018

2. Again, think about your business plan and forecast how your business might need to grow over the next twelve months or two years. What do you expect to be some of the technology, product, skills or opportunity impacts? How will this affect your team and resourcing requirements?

3. Just as in *Part 1: Hire*, this is a good opportunity to complete a SWOT analysis for your business, using the following grid as a guide. Once you have answered these questions you can use the SWOT analysis to develop strategies for achieving your business goals and generating contingency plans.

STRENGTHS	WEAKNESSES
• What advantages does your business have? • What do you do better than anyone else? • What factors mean that you get the sale? • What is your business's Unique Selling Proposition?	• What disadvantages does your business have? • What could you improve? • What should you avoid? • What factors lose you sales?
OPPORTUNITIES	THREATS
• What good opportunities can you spot? • What interesting trends are you aware of? • What changes in the market or industry can be used to benefit your business? • What gaps or needs in the market can you fulfil?	• What obstacles do you face? • What are your competitors doing? • What changes in the market or industry may have a negative impact on your business? • Do you have bad debt or cash-flow problems?

4. Considering your analysis, does your existing organisational structure still make sense? Are there any glaring omissions or opportunities to merge roles? Is one area top heavy, or over- or under-resourced? Are there opportunities for developing team members with multiple skills so they can cover other roles? This will reduce your exposure to attrition and enable you to effectively cover your annual leave schedule. This will also address the development desire of your employees and minimise financial impacts to the business.

5. Map out a new organisation with the roles and skills you need filled, those that can be merged, and those that are no longer relevant. Once you are clear on your final set of roles, it's time to write their job descriptions.

Phase 2 – Job descriptions

At the beginning of *Part 1: Hire* you wrote job descriptions for the roles you thought you needed. Now you're doing to review those against the actual roles you've created (and the ones you've realised you need as your business has grown).

Is it really that important? Yes! Now, before you fall asleep please hear me out.

Your business is going gang busters as you always knew it would. You're working at a hundred miles an hour and things need to get done, but you can only be in so many places at one time and you can only do so much. Sound familiar? You know, well at least you hope you do, what the end game is for your business. Now you need to communicate this, frequently and effectively to your team.

Your employees or team need to be very clear and understand exactly:

- What is expected of them
- What success looks like
- What their priorities are
- How their time should be allocated
- Who they report to
- What skills you need them to have to do their role

My concern has always been that sometimes business owners think that their team are mind readers and should just intrinsically know what is required of them. But how can they know this or, even still, remember it if it isn't written down? The mere physical process of writing the job description may allow you to reassess your thinking about what is required and the goals and interactions of the role in a different light.

When you have a number of employees, it is even more important to have clarity about who does what. With more people there is increased potential for confusion no matter how much they love what they are doing. It is critical in businesses to get alignment on the ideal outcome. Job descriptions can help with this.

Job descriptions will make the work easier as people will know what they are doing, and you will know too. It is amazing to see the peace of mind that comes from everyone knowing what is expected of them and just getting on with it. Productivity will be increased, and you will have more time to get on with what you need to do. This does not have to dull creativity or initiative; these can also be skill requirements of the job description.

The other advantage of documenting roles and responsibilities is when a particular team member is not performing to the required level. It is very difficult to accuse them of not doing their job if they don't know exactly what that job is. It is somewhat irrelevant that you feel you have verbally communicated your needs and the tasks in hand. The tasks and responsibilities need to be in writing – such as in a job description.

> **TIP:** It is much more difficult to exit someone if their role and the tasks within that role have not been made clear and documented effectively.

1. Pull out your current job descriptions – are they still current or do they need to be reviewed? Are these job descriptions still describing what you need the roles to be?

2. Compare these descriptions to your new organisation chart – are all the roles represented? Are some of them no longer necessary, or have some of them merged? Is a new role required to fill a gap?

3. Archive the job descriptions that are no longer relevant and, if you already have employees in those positions, consider where you can move them within the business using their existing skills (or how you can train them to fit into a new position).

4. Update any existing job descriptions with the new responsibilities that are required as you move into your next stage of growth and merge any existing job descriptions where necessary.

5. Finally, write new job descriptions for the gaps you found in your organisation chart. Going back over the roles that are no longer necessary, do you have any employees who could fill the new roles?

Phase 3 – Transition plan

The transition plan is far more important when you have existing employees whose positions may change, along with employees whose positions may have been made redundant.

The first thing you need to do is review your current and future states and plan how you will transition over time to the future state.

1. Evaluate your current team by using the 9 Box Grid Method. This can be a simple way to review your team in terms of their performance and perceived potential. This can also help you think through who you want to invest in, whose performance needs improving, and who you want to exit.

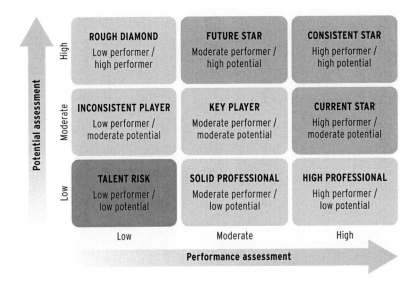

2. Consider your organisational plan, the new positions you want to make available, and the positions you want to make redundant. Rather than replacing attrition in an over-resourced team, look to develop the skills of a current employee to take up a new role or look to make some roles redundant. In the case of roles that are merging or growing, your 'stars' will be your first choice. In the case of roles that are becoming redundant, if those employees are decent performers or have high potential, see if you can redeploy them to other roles in the business.

3. Conduct quarterly reviews against your transition plan to check on progress and adjust as required.

Phase 4 – Managing the transition

In any workplace, change is a consistent presence and businesses that can react quickly and effectively to manage the change will have a distinct competitive advantage.

In the past, managers held the view that they would just dictate a change, and everyone would magically embrace it, but this is not the case. Leaders who understand change and work within a change management framework effect change more quickly and can introduce lasting changes into their workplace.

To understand how to manage change you first need to understand the reaction your employees may have. The following emotional cycle is based around the work of Elizabeth Kubler-Ross: starting with denial, 'It won't really happen'; followed by resistance, 'Surely I can stop this'; followed by exploration, 'I think I need to know more about this'; and lastly commitment, 'I understand the change needed and what I need to do to make it successful'.

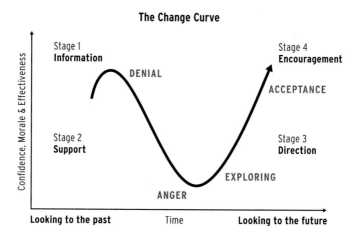

The Change Curve

Identify employee reactions

To figure out where your employees sit as you transition, look out for these behaviours:

Denial

- Avoid the topic
- Refuse to take initiative
- Act like nothing is happening
- Only do routine work
- Appear unconcerned

Resistance

- Show anger
- Complain and blame
- Become passive
- Become exhausted and overwhelmed
- Often become preoccupied with the change

Exploration

- Experiment
- Seek new ways
- Begin to see the future possibilities
- Take risks
- Have trouble staying focused

Commitment

- Sense they are in control
- Are comfortable
- Take time to affirm and recognise their efforts
- Reflect on what they have learnt
- Start looking ahead to the next change

Manage the change

The best way to manage your transition (or any change in business) is by following these steps:

1. **Understand**

   Understand what the change is and why you are looking to introduce the change. What are the expected benefits? Who will the change impact? How do we know if we have been successful? What are the risks and how can we manage them?

2. **Plan**

   How are we going to take employees on the journey? How do we prepare them for the change? What do we need to communicate? What training needs to be delivered to assist with the change? What are the key messages?

3. **Action**

   Have we asked people how they are feeling? Do they have ideas they can contribute? Do individuals know why the change is happening? Are we managing risks effectively? Is the communication strategy supporting the change?

4. **Embed**

   Did we achieve the benefits we were expecting? Are we sharing our success stories to reinforce the positive aspects of the change? Is there still resistance and, if so, how is this being managed? Provide resources for the change.

Deal with resistance

If you are experiencing resistance to the change, there are three ways to combat this:

1. **Empathy and support**
   Recognise and acknowledge how people are feeling. Use active listening to hear their concerns and ensure that they know that you understand.

2. **Communication**
   If people don't have enough information the gap will be filled with rumours and gossip. Employees are generally more comfortable if they know the worst news rather than nothing. Communication can help people prepare realistically for the change.

3. **Participation and involvement**
   The best way to reduce resistance to change is to involve employees in planning and implementing the change. The benefits are two-fold – the solution is high quality, and, because of their involvement, resistance is lowered.

Before you roll out a big change remember, people are people and you will go through these stages every time, whether you like it or not.

> **TIP**: Communicate, communicate, communicate – you can never over communicate about change.

'FIRST RULE OF LEADERSHIP: EVERYTHING IS YOUR FAULT' – A BUG'S LIFE

The reality of running a small business is that you never switch off. It is not a job; it is more of a calling – one where you 'make hay while the sun shines'. A business owner is constantly thinking about their business. As such, day-to-day operational pressures – ensuring stocks are managed appropriately, focusing on business development, addressing resourcing issues, and more – tend to take priority over thinking about how you're behaving as a leader.

However, when it comes to managing your employees, you *are* their leader and your behaviour is something you need to be conscious of if you want to get the best out of them and the best out of your business.

While many large organisations spend a lot of time (and money) focusing on developing future leaders – and consultants the world over are grateful for this – the reality is that having a strong leader within a small- to medium-sized enterprise is even more critical.

As a leader, you are the role model that others in the organisation look up to and emulate. If you are unclear on what your organisation stands for (your values), how your organisation is going to compete in the market place, how others in the organisation will be treated and so on, then the employees in your organisation will be unclear on how they, in turn, are expected to behave.

The main risk of poor leadership is increased employee turnover and the associated costs involved with re-hiring, re-training and bringing employees back up to the required level of productivity, which can vary from 50% to 150% of their annual salary, depending on the complexity of the role.

There is an old and well-known saying that people join organisations and they leave managers (leaders). This still holds true. If your employee turnover is high, first look to yourself and reflect on why they are leaving and if there is anything you could be doing differently to decrease these occurrences.

What type of leader are you?

There are many types of leaders and I am sure that you personally have come across many of them. I believe that business owners do not put enough thought and development into their role as leaders in their businesses. Take this short quiz to reflect on your perceived leadership style:

1. How would you describe your leadership style?
2. How would your team describe your leadership style?
3. How would your clients describe your leadership style?

One of the most common ways to classify leaders is to look at the style of behaviour they demonstrate. These styles can broadly be classified as Laissez-faire, Autocratic, Participative and Bureaucratic.

Laissez-faire

A laissez-faire leader doesn't directly supervise employees and fails to provide regular feedback to those under their supervision. Highly experienced and trained employees requiring little supervision can perform well under the laissez-faire leadership style. However, not all employees possess those characteristics. This leadership style hinders the development of employees needing supervision and produces no leadership or supervision efforts from managers, which can lead to poor productivity, a lack of control and increasing costs.

Autocratic

The autocratic leadership style is where managers make decisions alone without the input of others. Managers possess total authority and impose their will on employees. No one challenges the decisions of autocratic leaders. This leadership style benefits employees who require close supervision. However, creative employees who thrive when collaborating in groups detest this leadership style.

If a leader tends to micro-manage and be autocratic, the employees will default into a 'do as you're told' mentality and will be unlikely to expend discretionary effort for the organisation.

Participative

Often called the democratic leadership style, participative leadership values the input of team members and peers, but the responsibility of making the final decision rests with the participative leader. Participative leadership boosts employee morale because employees make contributions to the decision-making process. It causes them to feel as if their opinions matter. When a company needs to make changes within the business, the participative leadership style helps employees accept changes easily because they play a role in the process. However, this style can meet challenges when companies need to make a rapid decision.

Bureaucratic

Here the leaders strictly adhere to organisational rules and policies, and they make sure that their employees also strictly follow those procedures. Promotions take place based on an employee's ability to adhere to organisational rules. This leadership style gradually develops over time and is most suitable when safe work conditions and quality are required. However, this style discourages creativity and does not make employees self-contented.

What makes a good leader?

Hmmm, a perennial question. As with most things it depends
on the situation – many people would say that Steve Jobs was a great
leader; however, a lot of people who worked with him described him
as tyrannical. In a similar vein, Lee Kuan Yew – the leader who drove
the transformation of Singapore from an entrepot trading hub to a
leading financial hub and first world country within forty years – was a
good (if not great) leader. However, his style could be perceived as more
autocratic than democratic or participative.

One way to view good leadership is to consider the type of leadership
that would be most appropriate given a specific situation. The best-known
approach to deal with this is called Situational Leadership Theory
(Hershey and Blanchard) and explains the style of leadership that is most
appropriate depending on the degree of competence and commitment.

Situational approch to leadership
Managerial leadership styles

SUPPORTING PRAISE, ESTEEM & FACILITATE For people who have > High competence > Variable commitment	**COACHING** DIRECT & SUPPORT For people who have > Some competence > Some commitment
EMPOWERING TURN OVER RESPONSIBILITY FOR DAY-TO-DAY DECISION-MAKING For people who have > High competence > High commitment	**DIRECTING** STRUCTURE, CONTROL & SUPERVISE For people who have > Low competence > High commitment

High ← Supportive behaviour → Low

Low ← Directive behaviour → High

Adapted from **Leadership and the One Minute Manager**, Ken Blanchard

The model can be slightly unusual to follow since it operates from right to left as it follows the typical development of an employee. So, let's take an employee who has just joined a business. In the beginning, they will most likely require the directing style of leadership since they don't know what they need to do. As their competence increases, the style of leadership required will move to the coaching quadrant. The leader will still need to be there and provide the guidance, but this will be less directive in nature than previously. As experience and competence increases further, the role of the leader becomes more supportive, where an even lighter touch is required. The employee knows what needs to be done and only requires a degree of praise and recognition to retain their engagement. Finally, in an empowering style, a leader can totally trust an employee to not only deliver on the technical competencies required of the role, but to also have a degree of commitment to the organisation. They can therefore be empowered to deliver results independently.

So, while Lee Kuan Yew may have been viewed as more autocratic and directive in nature, this was what was required of him as a leader at that point in time. While everyone needs a leader they look up to, admire and seek to emulate, different employees require varying degrees of leadership to be demonstrated. As times change, the requirements of leaders change. A good leader is one who is able to adapt their style to the requirements of the situation and the employees they are working with. While many leaders can do this, others who do not have this natural capability can develop it by taking the time to reflect on the individual they are interacting with and the impact they want to have on them, and then intentionally adjusting their interaction – without becoming inauthentic.

Instead, focus on being authentic.

Authentic leadership is a phrase that is most commonly associated with Bill George, the ex-CEO of Medtronic – a leading maker of medical devices that have significant and lasting impacts on improving the lives of their patients. The underlying principle of authentic leadership is that leaders have an honest relationship with their followers. They value their input and this relationship is built on an ethical foundation. Generally, authentic leaders are positive people with truthful self-concepts who promote openness. By building trust and generating enthusiastic support from their employees, authentic leaders can improve both individual as well as team performance.

Are there times when leadership is particularly important?

In times of change (either growth or downsizing), the need for a leader increases. One of my favourite sayings is, 'People can deal with bad news better than they can deal with uncertainty.' In times of uncertainty people require increased communication and clarity. If the organisation is growing, people are keen to understand where they fit into the company-to-be, and are generally excited about the future and the potential opportunities such growth promises. Similarly, if an organisation is performing poorly, then there is increased apprehension and concern, 'Will I lose my job?', 'How will I pay the bills?', and so on. The impact of the role of the leader in conveying calm, clarity, direction and belief in their employees is increased in comparison to a business-as-usual situation.

How can I improve my leadership skills?

There is a joke about psychologists – how many psychologists does it take to change a light bulb? ... One, but the light bulb really has to want to change!

In the same way, a leader who wants to improve their leadership skills must really want to change their behaviour. The best way to achieve this is to first undertake some form of assessment of your current style, underlying personality attributes, and characteristics or pre-dispositions that may undermine your ability to change your behaviour. The objective is to increase self-awareness so that there is increased clarity on what needs to change. Once you have clarity, you can then decide which area to focus on and take the necessary steps.

A simple framework here is Awareness, Acceptance, and Action. This chapter has focused on becoming aware of what makes a leader and if there is the need to change. Acceptance is up to you.

The next step is Action, which is the focus of the rest of *Part 2: Manage.* This part of the book focuses on how you can effectively manage employees, including chapters on:

- Policy – Consistent policies are the benchmark for your treatment of your employees, and your employees' benchmark for their treatment of each other. As far as your skills as a leader are concerned, putting policies into action ensures you treat your employees fairly.

- Training – From induction to improving their management skills, regular training meets your employees' need for growth, as well as meeting your business's need for multi-skilled, promotable employees.

- Engagement – The best leaders keep their employees engaged. In this chapter you'll learn how to create a culture where your employees are eager to go above and beyond the call of duty.

- Leave – Everyone needs a break some time, and it isn't as complicated as you think to manage effectively and accurately.

- Wellbeing – Here you'll learn how to keep your employees safe and healthy, and how to stay on the right side of Work Health and Safety regulations.

- Performance management – Part of being a leader is giving structured feedback, both positive and negative. In this chapter you'll learn how to tackle any performance issues that arise, while staying compliant and giving your employees the opportunity to improve.

- Communication – Communication is an essential leadership skill, and the foundation of managing employees. This chapter will teach you the basics, so you can confidently navigate any situation.

- Measurement – Finally, to improve as a business and to improve as a manager, you need to measure your results. Here you'll learn how.

TIP: What are some simple changes you can implement today to improve both your leadership skills and others' perceptions of them?

POLICY – SETTING THE STANDARDS FOR EMPLOYEE MANAGEMENT

If you are like most businesses, when you started out you had a vision for your business which may or may not have included employees. Your business has most likely grown organically and sometimes at a pace that you were not expecting. As a result, employee-related policies are often forgotten due to:

- A lack of time
- Being focused on the core business
- Being small enough to just communicate the process verbally
- A lack of knowledge
- A lack of awareness around legal obligations under employee legislation
- Fearing building in bureaucracy

However, employee policies are essential for any business for the following reasons:

- **Legal obligations** – With the hiring of employees comes numerous legal obligations; an example being that you have a duty-of-care obligation to your employees. Your employees also have obligations around Workplace Health and Safety to ensure that they follow safe procedures, but how will they know what these obligations are if they are not documented or communicated?

- **Obligations to educate your team** – If an employee raises a complaint of sexual harassment by another employee, and it can be shown you have not trained your employees in appropriate workplace behaviour, then you are at significant risk of breach and are liable for fines.

- **Consistency of approach** – As your team grows so does the complexity of your business. It is easier to have a consistent approach to annual leave applications rather than managing each request in a different way. Employees will quickly become anxious if they perceive favouritism or inequity in the treatment of individuals.

- **To enable performance management** – Performance management is a complex area (it even has its own chapter later this section) and needs to be managed carefully and in a procedurally fair way every time. It is very difficult to say to someone that they should not drink excessively at lunch and then return to work and talk to clients if you have never shared a drug and alcohol policy with them.

- **To scale** – When you are small it is so much easier to communicate by just chatting across your desks; you are available to answer questions readily and you will only be asked each question once or twice if you only have a couple of employees. Imagine having ten employees that don't know the way to claim expenses or apply for leave without you having to answer every question multiple times. This is not an effective use of your time. You should be aiming to work more on growing your business, not being buried in it.

- **Systemisation** – When you systemise your business, as in establishing processes and procedures, you make your business more attractive for sale. The sign of a successful business is that it can survive without you. What should be systematised? Anything that gets repeated. I even have a client who has a documented process on how to post a letter for business. (Which might be over doing it...).

Structure of a policy

When you draft your employee-related policies it is important to have a consistent format. That way employees can easily search, read and digest the subject and know what it means for them. I recommend the following framework:

1. Opening statement around the intent of the policy – What is the purpose of the policy and why do you have it?

2. Definitions of the terms used in the policy – For example, Annual Leave: the number of days of paid leave for holidays after a period of continuous employment.

3. Content – What are the details of the policy? What can, and can't an employee do? What is the process that they need to follow?

4. Approvals and review – Who is the author and when was the policy last reviewed?

Which policies do I need?

The reason why many small businesses avoid having policies is they feel that they don't know where to start and which ones they might need. I would recommend the following as the minimum required from a legal and pragmatic viewpoint. You can always add more, if required.

- Code of Conduct – Expectations of behaviour and consequences for poor behaviour

- Parental Leave – Both maternity and paternity

- Annual Leave – Balances and how to apply for leave

- Personal Leave – Reasons it can be taken and balances

- Discrimination, Sexual Harassment and Bullying – What constitutes a breach and the consequences of a breach

- Expenses – What you can claim and how

- Alcohol and Other Drugs – Management of alcohol and drugs in the workplace and testing policies and procedures

- Dress Code – The required dress code

- Annual Reviews – The process employees and managers are to follow

- Managing Grievances – How to manage a grievance so that conflict can be resolved effectively in the office

- Long Service Leave – What happens when employees meet this milestone

- Equal Employment Opportunity – What EEO is and what needs to be considered

- Information Technology – How IT should be appropriately used in the workplace

- Performance Management – Managing a non-performing employee

- Domestic Violence Policy – how to support and manage an employee experiencing domestic violence

- Mandatory Data Breach – how to assess and manage data breaches

If you would like to see examples of these policies, then please refer to the Employee Matters website at: employeematters.com.au under the *Hire to Fire toolkit* section.

Storing your policies

In the past, most employee handbooks or policies were shared in hard copy format but today it is much more effective to have these in a soft copy format on the company intranet or in a shared folder or drive. Policies should be readily accessible to all employees (but in a protected format, such as a PDF, so that no unauthorised changes can be made).

Usage

The best time to share your employee policies is with a new hire as part of their orientation. I would also recommend having each employee sign off that they have read, understood and agree to abide by the policies. This is important to establish if there is a subsequent breach.

If a policy has been changed or a new one added, it is good practice to circulate this across the team and request acknowledgement.

A word of caution here – *if you have a policy you need to follow it accurately.* The Fair Work Ombudsman will be most displeased if you have a policy but choose to ignore it or to use it only when it suits.

Review

I would recommend that you review all policies annually to ensure that they are still current, unless there is a change in legislation that needs to be addressed immediately, for example, the changes made in 2018 to the Mandatory Data Breach legislation.

WHAT IF THINGS GO WRONG?

Often the fundamental risks to a business are unknown until
they happen. The trouble is, that can be too late. From the simple
crashing computer to the full sweep of the financial markets, when
you haven't prepared for risks they can adversely affect your business
and your employees.

So how do you protect yourself, your team and your business?
What can you do to make it safe?

A few years ago, I was working for a corporate travel agency in
Sydney when someone cut the vast majority of the city from their power
and their internet (whoops). A travel business cannot function without
phones and computers. Losses were likely to happen quickly, especially
if travel was unable to be booked and therefore clients were not being
serviced. This business needed to get back online and quickly. They
arranged to hire space in one of the large hotels in an unaffected part
of the CBD and quickly set up a temporary office. Now there was no
way that all 100 employees could relocate to the small space that was
to be the office for the next couple of days. Decisions needed to be
made on the critical people who would run the business in contingency
mode. For those employees forced to stay away from the office, regular
communications needed to be drafted and sent.

Having a business continuity plan can ensure that all employees are
kept safe and that business can quickly resume even if initially operating
in 'safe' mode.

There are five steps – while each is simple, each is also critical to the
successful creation of an effective and worthwhile continuity plan.

1. **Identify the key risks your business faces** – This is the most important factor. You need to ensure that you know what the risks are, and then you can consider what you need to do to mitigate them. There are some risks that you may well not be able to mitigate or some that you will be happy to accept – it's not knowing what the risks are that can make or break your business. These risks can include key person risk – risks to the people who are the critical players in your business.

2. **Communication** (that old chestnut!) – Everyone should know what they need to do (or not do) in the event of a crisis, emergency or risk event. This involves clear cascading calling/communication. Everyone in the business should at least have the contact details of one senior colleague and one junior colleague. If, for example, the city was locked down after a terrorist event; you need to quickly and efficiently advise employees not to come to the city. To avoid misinformation in these cases, a clear call plan is paramount.

3. **Know what your critical processes are** – What are the processes and resources that you cannot do without? How long can you do without others? A day? Two? Or maybe a week?

4. **Key personnel** – Identify these and ensure there are cover and communication alternatives. Also ensure these individuals know who they, and the others, are.

5. **Testing** – Most businesses get a continuity plan written up then they tend to forget about it. It must be tested at least once a year and the results recorded and escalated to the top guys. The continuity plan should also be easily accessible and regularly reviewed to ensure it remains pertinent to the business.

TRAINING – TO BUILD GREAT TEAMS YOU NEED TO INVEST IN YOUR PEOPLE

If you really want your employees to hit the ground running and exceed your expectations, you need to have a structured training program. This starts with the induction and orientation on their first day, along with ensuring they're familiar with company policies.

Once they've settled in, you can focus on training them to perform at the best of their abilities, with general skills like problem solving, customer service skills, communication skills and systems skills.

Induction and orientation

About ten years ago I was seconded to work for a couple of months in India, maybe longer if I did a good job and liked it. I already knew the company well, as I had worked for them for seven years, but I did not realise that when I arrived, no one would know that I was coming, where I was going to sit or what I was there to do. It was another three weeks before I met with my local manager to confirm the remit of the role. For many people, this situation would have been enough to send them home.

This is where many employers let themselves down. The first couple of weeks in a new role can be extremely unsettling and your new hire is already at a high risk of resignation. The best way to combat this is to have an effective induction and orientation program. Here are a couple of program imperatives:

- **Welcome and introductions** – Making employees feel warmly welcomed can go a long way to reducing the risk of a resignation. Make sure that you reach out to the new hire on their first day to welcome them and let them know that you are pleased they have joined the business. Ensure that you take the employee around to meet the whole team. This activity breaks down barriers and helps employees know who does what and where to go for help. Consider having a morning tea with the team to allow for some informal relationship building. This is also a way to facilitate information communication across team members.

- **Desk set up** – Ensure that their workspace is set up and cleaned for them, *before they arrive!* The worst way to welcome someone is to place them on a desk that still has all the previous employee's files, stained coffee cups and photos. Share some stationery with them and tell them how to get more stationery to get them started.

- **Induction training** – Depending on the size and complexity of your business this might be an hour or a full-day session. This training covers off:

  - An overview of the business and the departments
  - Marketing
  - Employee policies and processes (appropriate behaviour, how to apply for annual leave, etc.)
  - Culture
  - Customer approach
  - Office tour
  - Product overview
  - Workplace Health and Safety
  - Security and compliance
  - Information technology (company email, login details, appropriate use of internet, etc.)
  - Q&A

- **Handover** – Look to have a well-prepared and documented handover document for the new hire to refer to when they need to. Make sure that you have had another employee check it to ensure that it is correct.

- **Buddy** – Setting up a new hire with another employee as a buddy can be a great way to help to settle the individual and help them get up to speed quickly. This can be someone that they can ask the 'dumb questions' without feeling exposed.

- **Check in** – Make sure that you build in time to catch up over a cup of tea or coffee to see how the individual is settling in. Ask questions such as, 'Is your technology working for you?', 'Has the team made you feel welcome?', 'What has surprised you in your first couple of days?', or 'Are there any aspects of your role that you are finding challenging now?' I would recommend that the direct manager checks in formally at the end of the first week, first month, first quarter and finally at the six-month mark. This is also a great source of information for you.

Training in company policies

As discussed in the last chapter, the best time to share your policies is with a new hire as part of their orientation. However, in some cases it may be worth conducting regular training to ensure your employees remain up to date with how things should be done and what they can expect if they breach a policy.

Appropriate workplace behaviour

One of the best ways to not only improve the culture of your workplace while simultaneously reducing the likelihood of a bullying or sexual harassment complaint is to conduct annual training on appropriate workplace behaviour.

If you proactively take steps to educate your employees and act on inappropriate behaviour, it will also significantly reduce the size of any fine, should a case be proven against you. For many of us, we assume that it is obviously inappropriate to call your secretary stupid while meeting with a client (this once happened to me). Or, as happened when I left that office for the last time, to scream down the hall after me that I was a 'f*ckin' sl*t' for all the other office tenants to hear. For others, this might need to be made more obvious.

Training can cover the impact of inappropriate behaviour on the individual, the team and the company. Topics to cover include:

- Legal responsibilities for the individual and the company

- What is Equal Employment Opportunity?

- What is considered to be an extension of the workplace (for example, an offsite company Christmas party)

- What is discrimination and sexual harassment?

- What is bullying?

- Steps to take if you are subjected to inappropriate behaviour

Proven bullying can cost a company up to $3 million in the most serious cases. And, for a minor breach, it can cost $50,000 under WH&S legislation. Yes – really. There was a 2010 case from a Hawthorn Café where fines totalling $335,000 were issued for the bullying of teenage waitress Brodie Panlock who later killed herself.

Beyond informing employees that bullying and inappropriate behaviour *isn't* acceptable, the training will help employees know what to do if they do experience these things. This helps to resolve the matter to the satisfaction of all parties without the complaint being escalated to Fair Work. It should also cover retaliation, should an individual raise a complaint, which can form a separate investigation. The Fair Work Ombudsman now has the power to place an order on your workplace for the behaviour to cease immediately.

The challenge for businesses is that employees are very aware of their rights and will more readily stand up for them.

Workplace Health and Safety

Under Australian Workplace Health and Safety (WHS) law, a primary duty of a business is to put into effect a workplace safety management system. The system should incorporate the safety policies and safe operating procedures developed by your organisation in response to a thorough assessment of risks and hazards specific to your workplace.

A breach of the WHS legislation can incur fines of up to $3 million, so it is critical to ensure that your team members understand their role and obligations, and your company culture reflects this. Every organisation is exposed to varying degrees and one of the ways that you can reduce this exposure is by training your team regularly and effectively.

A vital component of a safety management system is training.

Importantly, this should include the assessment of worker competency. Competency assessment involves the active process of assessing your workers' learning of the topic, to be certain they have understood the material delivered. Officers of a PCBU (Person Conducting a Business or Undertaking) should be certain that their workers are able to undertake their work competently at all times. In this context, workers include officers, managers, supervisors, health and safety representatives, and contractors.

It is worth noting that if you have contractors who attend your business or worksite routinely, they should also be trained by you.

This means that WHS training should be included in induction or orientation processes for all new hires. You also need to complete generic training for subjects such as safe lifting. Competency assessment of specific tasks is an essential training activity.

Business owners should be aware of the risk of being charged with an offence under safety laws if a worker or workers involved in an incident in the workplace were not trained or inducted in the task they were performing at the time of the incident.

Ensure that you establish a system for documenting all training program content, as well as the delivery of the training and the names and positions of attendees. The records should indicate if each attendee did or did not demonstrate competency in the topic addressed by the training session.

Make sure that your workplace trainers have demonstrated their own skill or proficiency in the subject matter they are presenting.

IT and social media

Technology is changing at a rapid pace and, as a result, the systems and tools that we have at our disposal in the workplace are also changing rapidly. It is important that employers train their employees regularly on how to manage technology in the workplace.

One example includes protecting customer information and records, to abide by current data privacy laws. In this case, it is important to regularly remind employees about saving information on USB sticks or portable data files and managing this information effectively. Even hard copy information is at risk, as workers continue to take work home. Just imagine if some very sensitive data was left on a train seat during peak hour by a government official.

In the social media space, the lines are being blurred between what is a personal comment or activity and what is crossing over into the work environment. There have been cases where employees have made derogatory comments about their bosses or employers which have ended up in court and in the press. It is no longer a case of someone having a few too many drinks at the pub on Friday night and having a whinge about their boss – having this same rant on social media puts these comments in the public space, which can have major ramifications for both parties.

One example that happened to a client of ours was that they found the perfect male candidate, in terms of experience, and so made a verbal offer. The current team decided to check him out on Facebook only to find that his settings were public and that he had made some highly inappropriate comments about female genitalia. The new office he was joining was predominantly female, so based on these comments and their very public nature, the offer was rescinded.

Ongoing skill development in the workplace

Problem solving

Often the only difference between top athletes and others is what their coach brings to the equation. It is about bringing out the best in someone. Coaching for performance in the workplace works in the same way, but better.

Coaching for performance enables employees to come to the right conclusions themselves, thus owning the problem and solution. This is very empowering for people and is better received than being delivered as a fait accompli. Often, we intrinsically know the options and the likely best way forward, but we struggle with the assessment and decision process. Coaching can help with this and it is generally received very well by employees who experience this form of management.

My preferred coaching model is John Whitmore's TGROW model:

Topic – What needs to be discussed?

Goal – What goal or outcome is desired?

Reality – What is the current situation or reality?

Options – Explore all the options and their pros and cons.

Way Forward – Where to from here? Who is accountable?

An example might go something like this script: a senior manager, Tom, has a new employee, Sophia, who is not performing to the levels expected based on her interview, academic qualifications and references. Sophia has recently joined Tom's contact centre and is responsible for taking up to thirty calls per day providing IT advice. Tom calls Sophia into a one-on-one meeting.

> **Tom: (Topic)** *Thanks for coming to see me today, Sophia. We take our responsibility to effectively integrate you into the company very seriously, so today I would like to have a chat with you about how you are settling in and how you think you are performing, given your short time with us. Is that okay with you?*
>
> **Sophia:** *Yes of course.*
>
> **Tom: (Goal)** *We want to set all our new hires up for success so that they are performing at the optimal level as soon as possible. (Reality) So given that you have been with us for six weeks now, tell me how you think you are performing at the moment?*

Sophia: (Reality) *Umm, I think that I have done okay. I know that the clients like me as I have received that feedback from them directly and they seem happy when I am talking with them.*

Tom: *Yes, I have heard that during the quality assessment recordings. So, is there anything else that you feel that you are doing well?*

Sophia: (Reality) *I am getting along well with the other team members, well most of them. They are a great bunch and they have made me feel very welcome.*

Tom: (Reality) *You said most of them, is there someone that you are not getting on so well with?*

Sophia: (Reality) *I don't really want to say. I don't want to cause any problems.*

Tom: (Reality) *Sophia, I want to help you and it is important that I understand what is happening on the floor. Otherwise I can't help. What is the problem? Maybe we can work out how to solve it together.*

Sophia: (Reality) *Well is it Maria (team leader), she never seems happy with me and I think that it is because I am not able to solve the technical issues around Outlook as quickly as she thinks I should. When this happens, she gets frustrated and everyone can see that she is cross with me. Then I get nervous and find it harder to do my job.*

Tom: (Reality) *Why do you think that you are not solving the Outlook issues quickly enough?*

Sophia: (Reality) *Well, during the orientation training when this was covered I missed a day due to illness. Even though I have read the notes, I don't seem to get it.*

Tom: (Options) So what are some ways that you can think of to fix this situation?

Sophia: (Options) Well I guess I could review my notes again?

Tom: (Options) What would be the advantages and disadvantages of doing that?

Sophia: (Options) It would refresh my mind, but it hasn't helped to date.

Tom: (Options) What else could you do? And what are the pros and cons of that choice?

Sophia: (Options) I could ask Frankie, who is a whiz at Outlook, to see if she would be happy to give me some tips. This could work because I really like Frankie and I feel comfortable with her, but on the flip side Maria might get angry because I have not asked her for help.

Tom: (Options) How might you handle Maria then?

Sophia: (Options) I suppose that I could talk to her to let her know that I know Outlook is a problem area for me, but I want to sort it out and Frankie has agreed to help me.

Tom: (Options) How do you think Maria might feel about this?

Sophia: (Options) I suppose it is one less thing for her to think about and I have taken ownership of the problem, plus I know that she thinks Frankie is a talented operator.

Tom: (Options) What else could you do?

Sophia: (Options) I know that there are some online tutorials that I have not had a chance to review yet. I suppose I could do some of these in my lunch hour or when the phones are quiet.

Tom: (Options) *Great. What will this achieve for you, and are there any barriers that you can see?*

Sophia: (Options) *It shows initiative and also that I am willing to work on this in my own time. The downside is that I might have to miss a few lunch breaks while I catch up.*

Tom: (Way forward) *So given all your options, what are you going to do?*

Sophia: (Way forward) *Well I guess I will reread my training notes and then contact Frankie and ask for help. Then I'll let Maria know what we are doing and schedule some time in my diary for extra training at lunch or after work.*

Tom: (Way forward) *Sounds like a plan. How are you going to ensure that you do what you say you will?*

Sophia: (Way forward) *I was thinking that I might also ask Frankie to set me a mini exam at the end of two weeks to see if I have improved. What do you think?*

Tom: (Way forward) *I think that you have it all sorted, and I will look forward to our next catch up to see how you are getting on.*

Sophia: (Way forward) *Thanks Tom, I really appreciate your help and support.*

Tom: (Way forward) *My pleasure. Any time Sophia.*

Many employers may feel that this script takes a longer time to get to the same outcome than if Tom had just told Sophia what to do. But this way Sophia owns the problem and the solution and has begun to develop a positive and trusting relationship with Tom. I would argue that, although the initial conversation might take longer, the outcome or change will happen much more quickly and be more lasting. This is why managers with the ability to coach and encourage their employees typically get better results, including higher levels of productivity and performance.

Customer service skills

Your customers are the lifeblood of your company and their satisfaction and loyalty are instrumental to your success. As Henry Ford once said, 'It is not the employer who pays the wages. Employers only handle the money. It is the customer who pays the wages.'

The challenge can be that not all your employees will understand customer service to the same level, nor will they serve customers at a consistent level. It can be very effective to articulate your service standards and how you wish your customers to experience your business through employee training. For example, you want them to handle complaints in a way that makes your clients love you even more, despite an initial problem.

Effective communication skills

Teams with excellent communication skills are more likely to become high-performing teams. Communication skills can include active listening skills, body language and ways to ensure that communication is concise, understood and effective. Research has shown that 75% of oral communication is misunderstood, ignored or quickly forgotten. Imagine what the impact might be to your business if you could reduce this percentage to 50%.

Systems skills

Technology is an enabler but, if users are not trained effectively, technology can hinder a business and its employees. Steve Jobs once said, 'Technology is nothing. What's important is that you have faith in people, that they are basically good and smart and if you give them the tools they'll do wonderful things with them.'

During orientation, make sure that your new hires know how to use the technology that is used in your business.

To build a great team you need to invest in your people with training. From a legal perspective, ensuring they're aware of and abiding by all company policies will help reduce any potential minefields down the line. From a growth perspective, a training program will help keep your employees engaged and effective as you meet their desire to learn and develop.

ENGAGEMENT – WANT AN EXTRA 20% PROFIT THIS YEAR?

Why do some people want to desperately work for some businesses and avoid others like the plague? It's called engagement.

Employee engagement is 'the extent to which employees feel passionate about their jobs, are committed to the business and put discretionary effort into their work', according to Custom Insight, a leading company that develops online HR assessments and development tools. Engagement could also be referred to as an employee's motivation, or their willingness to go above and beyond the call of duty to get their salary at the end of a week.

For entrepreneurs, our engagement levels are extremely high; otherwise we would never achieve what we do on a daily basis. In your company, engagement might manifest itself by an employee regularly going above and beyond. They might actively promote your product or service, coming to and going from work with a smile on their face. When disaster strikes, they might be there at 11pm helping, because they believe in you, your business and their place in the company.

Engagement is different to employee satisfaction, which measures how happy or content your employees are.

Businesses that can make changes to improve their employee engagement will see positive results on the bottom line. Organisations with the highest levels of engagement outperform others in every commercial metric. Specifically, employers with over 80% engagement have reported:

- Increased productivity
- Increased customer satisfaction

- Increased ability to attract talent
- Increased customer loyalty
- Increased profit percentage
- Improved employee retention
- Higher sales and turnover

So how do you create engagement among your employees? Part of it comes down to having the basics in place – you need to be a good leader, you need to have clear policies, and you need to provide training so they can confidently work to the best of their ability. However, to really create a passionate workforce, you also need a great culture.

If I was to mention the brands Virgin, Zappos and Apple, what comes to mind? How would you describe those businesses, and what do you think it would be like to work there? How would it feel when you walked around their offices? What would the vibe be? What you are thinking, and feeling is the *culture* of these organisations.

Recent research shows that employees don't only want to work for authentic leaders, they want to work for authentic organisations. When a business focuses on its cultural strategy, many of the other metrics such as performance, productivity and engagement increase as a result. Attrition should also decrease as a result.

One of the massive benefits that you have as a business owner is the ability to determine, design and influence the culture of your business. So how can you do this? You can break it down into these three key areas – company identity, people and leadership.

1. Company identity

A great culture starts with a vision statement, a mission statement and your core values. These guide a company's actions and provide it with purpose. That purpose, in turn, orientates every decision employees make.

Vision statement

Your vision statement creates a long-term destination for your business – how do you want to be remembered? It declares the purpose of your company and serves as the standard against which employees, clients and suppliers weigh your actions and decisions. It is about what your organisation is aiming to become.

When they are deeply authentic and prominently displayed, good vision statements can even help orient customers, suppliers and other stakeholders. This means your vision statement is a simple but fundamental element of culture.

Ford Motor Company's vision statement is, 'One Ford'. This is a very clear message about where they are heading.

Mission statement

Your mission statement is the framework for your vision. The mission statement of a business or organisation is what they do.

Ford's mission statement is, 'One Team, One Plan, One Goal'.

If you don't have either a vision or a mission statement, I suggest you work with your team to develop these. The wonderful outcome is that your team will love being involved and will really embrace the vision and mission as a result.

Core values

Your core values define the attitudes and behaviours that will be required of your employees to make your vision and mission a reality.

At Employee Matters, our core values are:

- **Authenticity & Integrity**
- **Commerciality**
- **Experts in our field**
- **Long-term Partnerships**
- **Flexibility**
- **Employees Matter**

I often say to my team that this is the lens that we place over everything we do. This is particularly important to my team and I because we are a remote team. I want to be sure that when my team are out with clients they are behaving in a way that is consistent with our core values at all times.

Your narrative

Every company has a unique history, a unique story. And the ability to unearth that history and craft it into a narrative is a core element of culture creation. The elements of that narrative can be formal – like Coca-Cola, which dedicated an enormous resource to celebrating its heritage and even has a World of Coca-Cola museum in Atlanta. Or it might be informal – like those stories about how Steve Jobs' early fascination with calligraphy shaped the aesthetically oriented culture at Apple. Either way, narratives are more powerful when identified, shaped, and retold as a part of a firm's ongoing culture.

The value of telling stories is in their impact. Valerie Khoo, founder of the Australian Writers' Centre, says, 'They're powerful because they package data, logic and analysis into an easily digestible form – easy to tell, easy to remember, easy to understand and, ultimately, easy to share.' Your business story will help your clients understand what your business is about, what you do and maybe why you do it.

Your narrative is a part of how your vision, mission and values come to life. Where did you start? What was the journey you took to find your vision and mission? How have your values guided you? How do they tie into the business you want to become? All these elements form your business's narrative.

Find your company identity

To get started, consider the following questions:

- How do you want to be remembered as a business?
- What do you do?
- What does success look like?
- What is the long-term destiny for your business?
- How would your clients describe you and your team, and how do you *want* to be described?
- What's your business's story?

Remember – talk is cheap

Remember, your vision, mission and values aren't simply words on your website. They must be enshrined in your company's practices. If a business professes, 'people are our greatest asset', it should also be ready to invest in people in visible ways. Whatever your company's values, they must be reinforced in review criteria and promotion policies, and fully lived and incorporated into the operating principles of daily life in your business.

If you express your values, vision and mission through giving back, even better! Employees want to know that they are doing something more than just making you and your business money. Identify a charity or a cause that your company supports – not just one so you can say you give to charity – choose one that is deeply aligned with your values, vision and mission.

At Employee Matters, we support B1G1 – Business for Good. With B1G1, more than 2,300 businesses from forty-three countries have made 150+ million impacts. We believe that through working with B1G1 we can make a real difference in our world together.

At the time of writing, Employee Matters has created 130,962 Giving Impacts, predominantly in the area of health. One way that we use this, is at Christmas time, when we ask our team to select the projects that we should donate to. Instead of giving Christmas cards to our clients, the money we would have spent goes to these great causes. Last year, we could not decide between buying goats for villages or providing orphanage mums for children's homes in Cambodia. So, we did both.

2. People

Your business is only ever going to be as good as your employees. *Whether you like it or not, you are in a war for talent, which you need to win.* With the economy improving, the previous minimal rates of resignations are about to change and people with more confidence and more employability will start to look to move. Average turnover has been sitting at about 20%, but this is likely to increase.

The people part of your culture equation starts with hiring people who either share your core values or possess the willingness and ability to embrace those values. That's why the greatest firms in the world also have some of the most stringent recruiting policies. One study found applicants who were a cultural fit would accept a 7% lower salary and departments with cultural alignment had 30% less attrition. People stick with cultures they like and bringing on the right culture *carriers* reinforces the culture a business already has. For more information on hiring the right people, return to *Part 1: Hire*, particularly the recruitment process in *How to find the right people.*

For both your existing employees and new employees, there are a number of things you can do to increase their engagement and satisfaction, which will, in turn, create a better culture.

The package

When it comes to keeping employees happy and engaged, the most obvious place to start is by paying competitively. Know what your competitors are paying and where you sit in the range. While compensation is not the only factor employees consider when choosing to take (or leave) a role, it is important.

To sweeten the deal, think about other bonuses you could include in their package. One option is paying for an employee's or their family's private health cover, which can be very attractive to employees with families. Another is covering employee flu vaccinations. This has two benefits for the individual – a small monetary value and it gets taken care of during their working hours. For you as the employer, the more employees that have the injection, the fewer sick days are taken across the business overall.

Reward and recognition

Beyond the base package, to attract and retain the best team you can afford you need to consider reward and recognition. Why? Your team will be even more productive if they feel that their efforts are acknowledged and appreciated.

A couple of years ago, I won a small contract involving a six-week assignment to build a client an HR library containing some policies and procedures. After I arrived, they saw what I could do, and they had the idea of helping some of their smaller partners with HR support. The next thing I knew I was pitching for a recruitment assignment to hire sixty tri-lingual contact centre employees for a business partnering with Visa.

I will never forget when, after finishing the assignment, I was called out in front of the entire company as having made a substantial difference to the business. Yes, it was wonderful to see the growth of my department from inception to a big team but being publicly acknowledged made me feel like all the extra hours were worth it. (Now for someone else, this type of public praise could be an excruciating experience. So, you need to know your team and try to understand what they most value).

There are many forms of reward and recognition and it is a useful exercise to find out what employees value so that you can meet these desires. Not all of these programs are costly (believe it or not, compensation typically lands about fourth in the list of reasons for leaving an organisation).

Here are some examples of ways to reward your team:

- **Pay rise** – Most small businesses have a very haphazard approach to pay rises and very few seem to review annually. It is important that you know what the market rate is and, more importantly, what your competitors are paying. At the very least, you need to ensure that you are meeting the Modern Award minimums.

  Additionally, as the cost of living goes up stagnant salaries have less power in the real world, so it is worth considering how this impacts your team.

  Finally, performance-related increases are a great way to encourage greater productivity. You should definitely consider a pay review when you promote an employee into a more senior role. I have seen businesses withhold pay rises until the next review while expecting the employee to perform at the higher level. It is much more motivating to get a promotion and a pay rise simultaneously.

- **Bonus** – A discretionary cash bonus is a great way to instantly reward a result or behaviour. It is useful because unexpected rewards make a great impression and for the business it is a one-off, not an ongoing cost.

- **Awards** – One organisation I worked for had a quarterly HERO award that was nominated by peers or internal customers. This was a great way to publicly acknowledge behaviours that may have otherwise gone unnoticed by management. It is a great way to encourage the culture of 'helping out a mate'.

- **Spontaneous awards** – Think about a Red Balloon or an iTunes voucher, depending on your employee demographic, or suggest that an employee who has been working lots of extra hours takes their partner out for dinner to their favourite restaurant at your expense.

- **Praise or a simple thank you** – A smile, praise or a simple thank you costs nothing but it can make an incredible difference. Acknowledge your employees for their work and efforts. Praise can be public or private. While most people enjoy public praise, know your employees – if this will not work for them, don't do it.

- **Flexibility** – If a team has been working really hard, give them Friday afternoon off to go and do something that they enjoy. Some employers have a system where you can buy additional annual leave. This can work exceptionally well for working parents, in particular where vacation care can be expensive. One option is working forty weeks per year rather than the standard forty-eight weeks per year.

- **13th month of pay** – We have a client that, at Christmas time, has a discretionary 13th month of pay. Imagine how happy it would make your employees to receive an extra month's pay at one of the most expensive times of the year.

- **Promotion** – Many employees aspire to progress in their career and work their way up the ranks. Don't discount creating new roles that are positioned as a promotion to reward employees.

- **Company property** – Some employees love gadgets and to be in possession of the latest mobile phone technology or iPad can be a thrill. An added advantage is that they typically work longer hours with more access to technology. Just make sure that you have this logged as company property.

- **Share plan or profit sharing** – These are both great ideas but have significant tax implications, so it's best to speak to your accountant about this one.

These are just some ideas, but feel free to get creative – you can think of more, I am sure of it.

Opportunities for growth

Succession planning is not just for the big end of town – SME businesses also need to think about this. A key reason that people leave jobs is a lack of career opportunities or skills development. People want to grow and develop, so look for ways to continue developing your employees' skills. (And if you're thinking, 'What if we train them and they leave in a year?' Consider, what if you *don't* train them and they *never* leave?) Training is just as much an investment for your business as it is for your employees.

In small business, the ability to provide opportunity for growth can be challenging, but not impossible. On a small scale, consider paying for relevant qualifications on the proviso the employee passes. Zappos pays for non-relevant courses as well, such as massage therapy or music lessons, as one way to motivate employees. Their philosophy is that employees are total individuals, not just work personas, and by treating employees holistically they believe they get more out of them.

If you're ready to take a more holistic view, think of training from the point of view of career planning or succession planning. This is relevant at any time in your business journey and if you are transitioning to a new organisational structure (refer back to *Organisational development*) then it is more relevant than ever.

To get started, have conversations with your team to understand which other roles in the business may be of interest to them. This information can help you create experiences or opportunities that will help them move towards this goal.

Once you know they're interested in a certain area, focus on making them multi-skilled now, rather than waiting for a position to become available. One of the best ways that you can protect yourself against headcount fluctuations, illness or cost implications is to cross-train as many of your employees as possible. Don't wait for someone to be off sick. Proactively look to have team members learn each other's roles.

A tip here is that this will be significantly easier if each role has a job description (go back to *Organisational development* for more on this) and process document. Giving the process flow to someone who is not familiar with the role and having them attempt to follow the instructions is a wonderful test of that process document. This approach will quickly pick up any issues. The other advantage is that it means handover times are reduced as the incumbent can refer to the process flow document, rather than having to ask you every time they have a question.

Also, know that some of your team will be perfectly happy to remain in the same role and have no desire for progression. A word of caution – don't assume this will remain the case for all eternity. Check in occasionally to confirm, without pressuring the individual, that this is still the case. These people can become your rock and are filled with an incredible amount of company intellectual property, so make sure you're still looking out for them.

Beyond multi-skilling employees, a great way to create engagement is to construct career pathways for your high-potential and high-performing employees. One of the best bits of advice I received from my father, who was a director of a merchant bank, was to always make sure that I trained someone up to easily take over my role. That way I would always be easier to promote as there was a logical and easy replacement. This can initially seem counter intuitive, especially for those employees that are trying to build a reputation of being irreplaceable, but the benefit of planning a career pathway and up-skilling your employees is that it's easier to reward their hard work with promotions and more responsibility.

Many businesses have logical career pathways built into their model. For example, you might be a travel consultant trainee, then a domestic consultant, then an international consultant moving on to supervisor. There might also be another alternative to move into a groups or conferences consulting role.

Think through some logical role transitions within your business. You might even look to create a role to enable a pathway.

Providing support

If you have employees and they stay with you for a reasonable amount of time, you are likely to be exposed to their personal lives as well. They will not only be experiencing a career life cycle with you but also their own life cycle. Life issues that may affect your employees include:

- Relationships, engagements and marriages
- Relationship breakdowns and divorces
- Births

- Deaths
- Serious illnesses
- Financial hardships
- Substance abuse
- Gambling
- Suicide
- Redundancy
- Parenting

Employees are feeling more overwhelmed with life than they were even ten years ago. The sheer pace of life, the rate of change and new technology all add to this. As a business owner, you are not qualified to deal with some of these events, and in some cases, you wouldn't even be aware that they were occurring.

If you have an Employee Assistance Program (EAP) you can provide counselling support with professional psychologists when your employees need it. The benefits are:

- Your employees feel supported and valued

- Your employees are less inclined to need extra personal or annual leave

- Your employees can be referred on to other specialist services at their own cost, if required

- Your employees are less likely to resign

- Your employees are less likely to rely heavily on your or other colleagues' support

- Your employees will be more productive at work and are less likely to reduce their team's productivity

- Experts are available and accessible on a timely basis

- Your employees are likely to remain longer with a business that supports them

- You'll increase employee engagement

In a previous role, I was the HR Manager for a business where a popular member of a team committed suicide. The team was understandably shocked and devastated, but unfortunately some grieving team members started assigning the blame for the suicide on the employee's manager. This anger was starting to spread and needed to be brought under control quickly, as this was definitely not the reason. We had already arranged for some on-site counselling support, and with this approach we were able to address these concerns in a controlled and appropriate manner. This counselling was both confidential and paid for by the business.

Most EAPs have an initial set up cost and then you are only charged if your employees access the service. They are typically entitled to four to six sessions, capped at a cost of approximately $180 per session. Some employees will not require all the sessions available.

People usually seek out counselling when they feel anxious, depressed, stressed or bullied. Talking to a counsellor gives them a chance to work through the situation, often reducing the pressure and assisting them to identify a way forward or to develop some strategies for dealing with issues when they occur.

All sessions are kept completely confidential and you will only be aware that someone has accessed the service by receiving an invoice. That is, unless you have over ten employees, and then you receive some high-level reports that can help you support your employees better and address any work-related issues constructively.

Making work social

Your employees, especially your full-timers, spend a large portion of their week at work and many people want to have a social component to the workplace as well. Do you have a shared lunch on Fridays, Friday night drinks or an annual family BBQ? Is it okay to share a joke or what you did on the weekend? Do you acknowledge other cultures or religions?

There are plenty of ways you can make the workplace more fun and sociable, including:

- **Social clubs** – A social club might arrange events like Friday night drinks but start these early so that even employees who are racing off to collect children from childcare can catch up quickly and informally with their team. A Melbourne Cup day lunch, a ten-pin bowling event or even a family picnic day are all great ideas.

- **Social media** – Social media is an extremely powerful tool that can be used for both good and for evil, and for many younger employees it is a fundamental part of their lives. Allowing people access to their favourite social media channels during their lunch break will reduce the need to do this in the toilet cubicle, but do conduct social media training so you protect your business, and employees are aware of what is and isn't appropriate behaviour.

- **Lunches** – One business I used to work for would order takeaway for a Friday lunch and everyone would gather around their desks while munching through Indian meals or pizza. The added benefit of these events is the informal mingling and relationship development. Great ideas can be discovered or developed over a pizza and a giggle.

- Birthday cakes – Acknowledge people's birthdays or work anniversaries (say at the five- or ten-year mark). Coffee and cake is a great way to break down perceived or real inter-departmental barriers and increase collaboration.

Giving back

Many employees want to work for a company that supports a social cause, that's dedicated to making the world a better place. However, many are also passionate about their own causes, so one initiative would be giving every employee a charity day that they can use to help their charity of choice. They might choose to help out at Meals on Wheels or at a soup kitchen or, alternately, donate a day's salary to the charity.

Creating a great place to work

Why does Pixar have a huge open atrium, engineering an environment where business members run into each other throughout the day and interact in informal, unplanned ways? And why do tech firms cluster in Silicon Valley and financial firms cluster in London and New York? There are obviously numerous answers to each of these questions, but one clear reason is that place shapes culture. Open architecture is more conducive to certain office behaviours, like collaboration. Place – whether geography, architecture, or aesthetic design – impacts the values and behaviours of people at work. As Daniel Priestley said, 'your environment dictates your performance'.

The Steelcase Global Report shows that not only does employee engagement positively correlates with workplace satisfaction, and but workers who are highly satisfied with various aspects of their workplace also demonstrate higher levels of engagement. In other words, it's a virtuous cycle – engagement leads to satisfaction, and that satisfaction leads to higher engagement.

Yet, only 13% of global workers are highly engaged and highly satisfied with their workplace. The inverse is true as well: 11% of employees are highly dissatisfied with their offices and are also highly disengaged.

It is also interesting to note that The Towers Watson 2012 Global Workforce Study found that only two in five workers (39%) in the Asia Pacific region are highly engaged at work. The rest, three fifths of the workforce, are struggling to cope with work situations that do not provide adequate support and emotional connection. These workers are not consistently productive, and they lack the willingness to go the extra mile for their employers. The lack of employee engagement translates to a cost for their employers in terms of loss in productivity, lower work performance and high employee turnover.

Numerous case studies and research over the years have found that office design can impact the following areas:

- Customer attraction and attention
- Productivity, motivation and retention of employees
- Employee knowledge and skills
- Innovation and creativity
- Inviting and embedding cultural shifts

I have noticed that many of my female clients have gone to considerable effort to personalise their offices with the use of colour, themes and accessories. When I asked them about the thinking behind their design, they talked about wanting to have a space where they enjoyed spending time and felt inspired and creative.

When you think through your employee strategy you should give careful consideration to what will best motivate and reward your employees, to give you their best every day.

3. Leadership

Regardless of your vision, mission and values, and the policies you put in place to reward your employees, it all starts with you. The leader in a business is the one who stops policies and initiatives from just being talk – you enforce them by acting with them in mind every day. It's your responsibility to make sure the company culture you envisaged is flowing through every level of your business. Keep the channels of communication open – talk to your employees, know what their personal motivators are and try and address these. Sell the vision and get people enthused about coming on the journey with you.

Employees want to like, admire and trust the people they work for, so aim for authentic leadership by providing clarity of direction and purpose, and show that you are honest, open, approachable and sincere. Remember to adjust your leadership style to meet your employees' needs depending on where they are. While there is no one way of behaving with employees – since every employee is different – you need to be true to yourself. Some people feel they need to try and copy a great leader, but this generally doesn't work because your operating context is totally different. Rather than trying to be someone else, be true to yourself; think about how best to motivate your employees and be sincere.

Remember the saying – employees don't leave organisations, they leave managers – so learn how to be a great one.

While there are other factors that influence culture, these three areas – company identity, people and leadership – can provide a firm foundation for shaping your business's culture. Identifying and understanding them more fully in an existing organisation can be the first step to revitalising or reshaping the inherent culture in your business.

The results of a great culture

I really like this definition of culture from Investopedia.com: 'The beliefs and behaviours that determine how a company's employees and management interact and handle outside business transactions. Often, *corporate culture* is implied, not expressly *defined*, and develops organically over time from the cumulative traits of the people the company hires.'

So, what does it look like when you get it right?

Increased productivity

For SMEs, understanding productivity and how to increase productivity is critical. Julia Gillard said in 2009 'to truly unlock the productivity of our nation we need workplace leadership and the requisite culture and skills ... to encourage innovation, workplace engagement and co-operation in our workplaces.' In this sentiment I absolutely agree with her.

Companies with great cultures regularly experience increased productivity, therefore creating an active, positive and widely embraced culture within a small business can really assist you to build a successful and profitable company.

When a business has a great culture, one where employees love to come to work, love their jobs and where employees regularly go 'above and beyond' what is required of them, productivity is positively impacted. In a business with a great culture, employees will continue to look for ways to improve processes or reduce costs, thus having a positive impact on productivity. They have an attitude of continuous improvement and take personal responsibility for their work. Where individuals feel proud of their output and accomplishments and take ownership of their work, a business will see their productivity results trend upwards.

Increased customer satisfaction

Your clients will determine whether your business is a success or not. Their increased satisfaction is intrinsically linked to your business's success, so you need to love your clients and show your employees how to love them as well. As Michael LeBoeuf once said, 'a satisfied customer is the best business strategy of all.'

In a business with a strong and proactive culture, employees will take personal responsibility for a client's satisfaction with the service given. Rather than just respond to the request they will look for other opportunities to exceed service expectations. Say a client rings to get some details on their account and the employee realises that the client could be on a more suitable plan. Rather than accept the status quo, they will take on the extra work to make the required changes to impress the client and their manager. They possess the attitude that this action is for the good of the company.

Increased customer loyalty

With increased customer satisfaction comes increased customer loyalty. You want your customers to refer you to their clients, associates and friends. You want them to be talking about you at a BBQ on the weekend, positively spreading your value and message at absolutely no additional cost to you. One of the best techniques that I have learnt here is to 'delight and surprise' your customers. For example, if your client has been a loyal and well-paying customer for some time an enterprising business owner would give them something complimentary of value – maybe a free course or new product – before anyone else.

When considering the impact that a great culture has on customer loyalty, it is where employees look to develop more personal and meaningful relationships with long-term clients, they look to enquire after their clients' children or partners by name. They genuinely show an interest in the lives of the clients, such as following up on recent holidays or weekends of sport. Everyone wants to feel of interest. As relationships become more personal, it reduces the chance the client will leave you as they are also significantly invested in the relationship. In addition, if there is a problem, there is more goodwill in the account to draw on without losing the account.

I had an example with a client this week where the initial relationship began as colleagues in the early nineties, and after meeting up again recently they became a client. The reason they became a client more easily was there was already a relationship and trust had been built. However, there was a hiccup in the support that we had provided and a difference of opinion about what had been agreed between one of my team and the client. I reminded the client that a part of our culture is building long-term relationships. We also recognise that as part of the nature of this long-term approach, there may be conflict at times. To us, working through this conflict is the key to developing long-term, trusted and mutually beneficial relationships. I went on to confirm that we valued them as a client and very much wanted to continue to work with them. Again, I referred to the fact that part of our culture is building long-term partnerships. The client relationship was saved using culture at the centre of our approach.

Increased ability to attract talent

I have been saying it for years now – there is a war for talent and organisations need to stand out if they're going to attract top performers. Culture is one way to do this by creating an environment that is attractive to prospective employees who are passionate about both what they do and what you do. This way you will attract more employees who will help you deliver and improve your product and offering.

Think about it; you can have two businesses that deliver exactly the same product, but candidates want to work for, and employees happily stay at, one of them, while the other has candidates that turn down job offers, and attrition rates are high. Why is this? It comes down to culture.

When Adam Bryant of *The New York Times* interviewed Lazlo Bock, the senior vice president of people operations at Google in June 2013, he found when Google is recruiting a technical role, the individual needs to have some technical skill but they are much more interested in behaviours that will support Google's culture, such as:

1. Cognitive ability – the ability to learn

2. Leadership – the ability to step up to lead but also to defer to someone with a better idea

3. Humility and ownership – the ability to collaborate

4. Fierce position – the ability to take a position or opinion on something unless some further information comes to hand then to possess the willingness to change their position

5. No content knowledge – the ability to offer a fresh perspective

Hiring candidates who possess these behaviours helps to build and maintain the culture of Google.

Increased retention

Replacing a role due to attrition will cost you up to 150% of that role's base compensation, so obviously this is not something that you want to do, if possible. The second cost you face is the amount of time that a vacancy is left unfilled. You can calculate this by knowing the day rate cost of the role and then using this formula:

Day rate x Number of vacant days = Vacancy cost rate

Luckily for you, high levels of engagement reduce attrition. A recent global survey conducted by the Hay Group showed that the main reasons employees leave organisations are a lack of confidence in leaders, opportunities for career development, autonomy, supportive work environment and appropriate compensation. Fortunately, all these things can be addressed with your company identity, your people and your leadership. In other words, this can all be addressed by creating a great culture.

If someone does leave, conduct an exit interview (see *Exit interviews* in *Part 3* for more information) and use the feedback to make your business and your culture better. However, if you work towards creating a great culture, retention shouldn't be an issue.

Higher sales and turnover

Do your employees, even at the most junior levels, know how production is tracking week by week or month by month? Share this information; make a competition out of it. Look to set incentives for improvement ensuring that quality does not suffer as a result.

Traditionally, businesses have kept their employees in the dark, but employees respond really well to understanding the business and feel a sense of empowerment and ownership as a result. Where a business feels that, culturally, it is the right thing to do to share information with employees, the result is that the business gains employee buy-in. They feel a sense of responsibility to do their bit. They can see the impact their actions have on both the top line and the bottom line. A competitive desire to continue to improve results or even to compete against other departments will start to drive up results.

Sharing information helps build trust which is what most employees are seeking from their employers. Gone are the days where you are expected to keep employees in the dark because all the numbers are confidential.

For many employees, financial information is not well understood. Look to educate all your teams on what you mean by revenue, gross margin and fixed costs. It also helps to clarify the differences between forecasts and actuals.

Improved teamwork

I recently heard of a case where one of the members of the local fire brigade lost his wife suddenly in tragic circumstances. After her death, the rest of his team covered his shifts so that he could spend more time with his children, who so desperately needed his love and attention at that difficult time. In a company with a great culture, there is a real sense of camaraderie and a strong sense of looking out for your team.

LEAVE

Leave can often feel like a big headache for small businesses – the reason you started hiring was because you were swamped with so much work, and *now* they're going on holiday, or they've been called for jury duty!

Permanent employees are all entitled to various types of leave, and if there are issues around taking it, this can have a large impact on employee satisfaction and engagement. However, if you are aware of your obligations, you will be able to prepare in advance, to lessen the impact on your business and keep your employees happy, healthy and rested with essential breaks.

Long service leave

Believe it or not, long service leave still exists. All permanent employees are entitled to long service leave in accordance with the relevant state legislation. Employees become eligible after completing a prescribed period of continuous service – usually ten years or more with a single employer, except in the ACT where it can be taken after seven years. However, the payout of accrued long service leave on termination of employment is after seven years' service in VIC, QLD, SA, WA, TAS, NT. In ACT and NSW, the payout is pro rated after five years' service. (workplaceinfo.com.au/payroll/leave/long-service-leave-all-states-and-territories#table)

An employer may also direct an employee to take long service leave, but this depends on the state legislation, and notice is required. It is generally permitted with anywhere between one and three months' notice. (workplaceinfo.com.au/payroll/leave/analysis/direction-by-employer-to-take-long-service-leave--is-it-permitted#.W4Y6p2XVTto) Any employees who want to take some of their long service leave should request this in writing. You can then consider the request, but you are not obliged to approve the request if appropriate cover cannot be arranged for the specified period.

Some states' legislation, surprisingly, can allow employees to work for another company during their long service leave, as long as the new employment does not pose a conflict of interest. In WA, VIC, NT and SA this is not allowed

You can replace the employee temporarily with another employee, but the replacement should specifically be made aware of the temporary nature of the role. When the employee comes back they should be returned to the same position, responsibilities and seniority as before they left.

An employee can be terminated while on long service leave, but only for a legal reason such as redundancy, summary dismissal or where the employee has repudiated their contract.

Parental leave

Many employers view parental leave and having female employees who might actually take it very negatively, but it should not be so. I believe some of this attitude comes from a time when women took leave and then, when they were due to return to work, chose not to. These days, women are returning to work in record numbers and in record time. I went back to part-time work through necessity when my second child was just three months old, though I was lucky enough to be able to work from home.

Any permanent full-time or part-time employees with at least twelve months of continuous service are eligible for unpaid parental leave (this includes adoption leave). Casual and fixed-term employees may also be eligible for unpaid parental leave.

When the employee returns, they need to be offered a job, role or position which is comparable to the one they had prior to commencing parental leave.

This period of leave counts as continuous service.

Where it is considered inadvisable for a pregnant employee to continue in her current role because of illness, risk arising out of the pregnancy, or hazards connected with the role, she may temporarily transfer to a safer role. The employee must have a medical certificate stating that they are otherwise fit for work.

If a pregnant employee is eligible for parental leave, her initial parental leave may start at any time within six weeks of the expected date of birth. If she continues to work in the six-week period prior to the expected date of birth, her manager can request a medical certificate stating that she is fit for work. If she does not (or cannot) provide the medical certificate within seven days of the request, she will be required to start parental leave immediately.

After taking parental leave, employees are entitled to return to the position they were in immediately prior to going on parental leave. If that position no longer exists, the employee can return to an available, comparable role.

Employees may request in writing to return to work early from parental leave. These requests may be approved at your discretion.

Employees may request a flexible work arrangement when they return to work, such as returning to work on a part-time basis, job sharing, or flexible working hours. Such requests should be made in writing. You need to respond to these requests within twenty-one days. If you don't wish to, or cannot grant flexible working arrangements, you need to have a very strong business case as to why that option is not available, such as that it is likely to cause your business a significant financial burden.

Employees can also request an additional twelve months of unpaid leave on top of the initial twelve months leave.

Community service leave (including jury duty)

Community service leave generally falls into two areas – voluntary emergency management activities and jury duty (including attendance for jury selection).

Emergency management activities relate to those who volunteer for bodies such as the State Emergency Service (SES), Country Fire Authority (CFA) or the RSPCA (in respect of animal rescue during emergencies or natural disasters) and are being called up for an emergency. You don't have to pay your employees for this activity, but there is no limit on the time that can be taken, providing it is for engaging in the activity itself and for reasonable travel and rest time.

For more information, go to fairwork.gov.au/leave/community-service-leave

Jury duty involves the time spent in the jury selection process, as well as the time spent attending a trial. As an employer, you are obliged to release any employee summoned for jury service.

Employers cannot:

- Force employees to take leave, such as recreation or sick leave, while doing jury service (this includes the day they go to court for a jury summons)

- Dismiss, injure or alter an employee's position as a penalty for doing jury service

- Ask employees to work on any day that they are serving as jurors

- Ask employees to do additional hours or work to make up for time that they missed as a result of jury service

Employers can provide employees with letters giving reasons why it might be difficult for the business if they have to report for jury service. I have to say from my exposure to the individuals attempting to get out of their service that the judge was neither patient, sympathetic nor supportive of any of the appeals I witnessed. If the employee is excused from jury service this time, they may be called up again in a few weeks or months.

> **TIP:** Consider that this will happen at some point to you or an employee in your business and determine your approach in advance.

If you are trying to get out of jury duty, a naughty tip is to wear your most conservative suit and carry the Financial Review under your arm. I once shared this tip with a young guy who had just landed his first job in the mail room and was devastated to be called up for jury duty in his first week at the new job. He followed my advice and, while he was called out, he was rejected by the prosecution, so it worked.

Is jury duty paid?

Jury service is paid for employees other than casuals (check your state laws regarding payment for casuals). These employees are entitled to make-up pay for the first ten days that they are absent for jury service.

Make-up pay is the difference between any jury service pay the employee receives (excluding expense-related allowances) and the employee's base pay rate for the ordinary hours they would have worked (excluding separate entitlements such as incentive-based payments and bonuses, loadings, monetary allowances, overtime or penalty rates).

Before paying make-up pay, an employer may ask the employee to provide reasonable evidence:

- That they tried to claim jury service pay
- Of the total amount of jury service pay that has been paid (even if there was no jury service payment)
- Of the total amount of jury service pay that is still payable for the period (even if there was no jury service payment)

If the relevant state or territory laws provide more beneficial entitlements than the National Employment Standards in relation to eligible community service activities, those laws continue to apply. This may be particularly relevant for paid jury service. The allowance paid to jurors is not intended to be a substitute for a salary or wage. Many large firms continue to pay their employees a wage while they are doing jury service.

Domestic Violence Leave

Following a decision of the Fair Work Commission Modern Awards will be varied from one August 2018 to give employees access to five days of unpaid family and domestic violence leave each year. Family and domestic violence means violent, threatening or other abusive behaviour by an employee's family member.

Employees can take the leave if they need to deal with the impact of family and domestic violence and it is impractical to do so outside their ordinary hours of work. Reasons for individuals taking this leave may include (but are not limited to) taking time to attend court hearings, accessing police services or making arrangements for their safety or that of their family members.

Who does it apply to?

The new entitlement applies to all employees covered by an industry or occupation Award. It does not apply to employees who are covered by Enterprise Awards, State reference public sector Awards or other registered agreements.

WELLBEING – HOW TO STAY COMPLIANT AND HAVE HEALTHY EMPLOYEES

An innovative, well-run business continuously drills deep to explore and flush out better ways to optimise productivity, profitability, and employee and customer satisfaction.

But when it comes to safety management, the most competitive small businesses can be guilty of doing the bare minimum to get them across the line in terms of safety compliance. If you knew something of the recent Australian safety law requirements, you would realise that a minimalist approach just doesn't cut it anymore. All businesses, regardless of size or structure, must now do 'everything reasonably practicable' to ensure a safe system of work.

Recent changes to safety laws in Australia have substantially raised the cost of damages that a business can incur if found to be liable for prosecution. In fact, the maximum penalties under the Work Health and Safety (WHS) Act do not make for good reading, as the following table shows:

Type of offence	Maximum penalty for corporations	Maximum penalty for officers	Maximum penalty for workers
Category 1 - Breach of a health and safety duty involving recklessness as to the risk of death or serious injury or illness without reasonable excuse	$3,000,000	$600,000 or 5 years' imprisonment	$300,000 or 5 years' imprisonment
Category 2 - Breach of a health and safety duty which exposes an individual to death or serious injury or illness (without recklessness)	$1,500,000	$300,000	$150,000
Category 3 - Other breaches of health and safety duties	$500,000	$100,000	$50,000

Additionally, in a business that does not have a safe system of work, workers who get injured often have a disaffected commitment to return to work and the rehabilitation process. Injured employees can be left to languish at home or wither in modified work roles that have been poorly considered, while the business loses productivity and the employee loses motivation.

So, it *is* important to control work hazards – beyond reducing the likelihood of your employees being injured; you'll reduce insurance liability, manage work injury claims better, and ensure your employees *want* to return to work.

But let's try to avoid focusing on the disincentives.

For the average small- or medium-sized business that desires creating a safe place to work, there is a far greater incentive and reward when considering the positives that can come out of building a proactive culture of workplace safety awareness (not to mention the ability to expand their business opportunities through Government tendering, which will require demonstrated evidence of a safe system of work).

What is that incentive? Well it is really quite simple ... taking active, holistic care of workers, employees and every single person who enters your workplace is an effective way for business owners and leaders to promote higher quality work and make their businesses more successful and profitable.

And it starts and ends with your leadership culture.

A workplace that cares holistically for its workers means empowering all employees to think about the whole of the business – in this case, the safety aspects of the business. A workplace that cares will see employers demonstrating an authentic interest in everyone's opinions and everyone's needs.

If your business's beliefs, values, attitudes, underlying assumptions and behaviours are co-owned and shared by the people in your workplace, people will be more inclined to watch out for one another. Safety becomes the first, last and greatest contributor and beneficiary by providing the perfect vehicle for employers to demonstrate they genuinely care about their people.

So, the message for workplace safety is clear – businesses that establish high-performing cultures, where leaders can clearly name acceptable behaviour, prioritise safe operating procedures and ensure continuous improvement of their safety management system, operate far more safely than those that don't.

And, as luck would have it, high-performance leadership cultures generally perform better than others in a variety of business outcomes, of which only one is safety.

Where should I begin with safety?

Done well, safety culture or leadership culture is king of the workplace.

It is everything.

Positive leadership culture affects the safety of every person and every person's every action in every workplace, every moment of every day.

As an owner of a small business, you are the key behaviour influencer and are best positioned to establish a leadership culture. Responsibility for building effective safety culture starts and finishes with the business owner working and planning in close collaboration and consultation with workers.

So where to begin? The following steps apply to any and every type of business – blue collar, white collar, even no collar!

1. Understand 'She won't be right, mate!'

For starters, if you own a business, before you do anything else, kill off any and all evidence of the old-school 'she'll be right' attitude to safety.

This attitude is obsolete.

Doing nothing about safety, praying that nobody will get hurt, or even being *anti*-safety (for example, removing safety-specific equipment) is tantamount to business, legal and personal suicide. Having safety policies, procedures, rules and regulations that are ignored or, worse still, not promoted or brought to life in the workplace, is just as bad – and may even be worse – than doing nothing.

2. Be aware of the statistics[1]

In the period from 2003 to 2016, some 3,414 workers lost their lives at work. 186 Australians failed to make it home from work in 2013. In 2012, it was 212, and in 2011 the number was 228. In 2011 this equated to two deaths per 100,000 workers. These figures are truly shocking and while the numbers are falling, one death is still a death too many.

And this doesn't include work-related injury and illness in Australia. These were estimated to cost $60.6 billion in the 2008/09 financial year, a staggering 4.8% of GDP!

In 2009/10 an average of fifty-eight per 1,000 Australian workers reported a workplace injury. This meant the injured workers required up to ten days off work or, in some cases, more than ten days off work.

In 2014/15, there were 110,280 Workers Compensation claims for serious work-related injuries or illnesses, or ten serious claims per 1,000 employees.

---

1   Safe Work Australia, 2014

Data from the latest available data (2015-16) show that there were 104,770 serious claims, or 9.3 serious claims per 1,000 employees – a drop from the previous year of 7%.

Per hour worked, male employees had a 25% higher rate of claims for serious injury or disease than female employees, and incident rates of serious Workers Compensation claims increased with employee age.

The highest occupation incidence rates were recorded by labourers and related workers, (over *double* the rate for all occupations), while the highest industry incident rates were recorded by the Transport and Storage, Agriculture, Forestry and Fishing, and Manufacturing industries.

A typical serious Workers Compensation claim involves four weeks' absence from work. One quarter of serious claims required twelve or more weeks off work. One in five serious claims involved a back injury.

3. ***Know and understand the differences between the new WHS and the old OHS (Occupational Health and Safety) requirements[2]***

    Changes for former OHS Representatives, OHS Committees and authorised representatives include:

    - Different functions for Health and Safety Representatives (HSRs), Health and Safety Committees (HSCs) and WHS entry permit holders

    - Unions are still able to prosecute certain breaches

    - Increased union right of entry to include entry for the purpose of advising and assisting on WHS (with twenty-four hours' notice)

---

2   Workplace OHS, workplaceohs.com.au

- HSRs may issue a Provisional Improvement Notice and direct that unsafe work cease

- Workers are given the right to cease unsafe work

Your responsibilities

Your business must ensure, as far as is reasonably practicable, the health and safety of all its workers. Workers under the current WHS laws include:

- Employees
- Trainees
- Apprentices or work experience students
- Volunteers
- Outworkers, contractors or sub-contractors
- Employees of a contractor or sub-contractor
- Employees of a labour-hire company

This means, for example, you must provide the same protections to volunteer workers as you do to your paid workers. The protection covers the physical safety and mental health of all workers. While you do not have to guarantee that no harm will occur, you must do what you are reasonably able to do to ensure health and safety.

Factors taken into consideration include:

- The type of business
- The type of work
- The nature of the risks
- What can be done to eliminate risks?
- The location or environment

Minimising risks and preventing incidents

To minimise risk and prevent health and safety incidents, you must:

- Provide and maintain a work environment without risks to health and safety

- Provide and maintain safe plant and structures

- Provide and maintain safe systems of work

- Insist on safe use, handling and storage of plant, structures and substances

- Provide and maintain adequate facilities for the welfare of workers

- Provide information, training and instruction or supervision that is necessary to protect all persons

- Undertake audits of Chemicals and provide current Safety Data Sheets for these chemicals

- Manage health and safety risks

- Think about what could go wrong, and the consequences

- Manage risk, including:

  1. Identifying hazards
  2. Assessing the risks
  3. Controlling the risks
  4. Reviewing control measures

Case study[3]

A NSW employer was fined $80,000 after a worker reached through a small gap in a machine guard – in contravention of safe work procedures – and had his hand cut off. The worker became entangled in the machine's rotating payoff wheel and lost his right hand. It was surgically reattached, and the worker was successfully redeployed.

The Industrial Court heard that, while the working side of the machine was guarded with an interlock gate, the worker regularly reached through a 393mm gap on the other side to remove caught tie wires and tags.

The employer pleaded guilty to failing to adequately guard the wiredrawing machine at its mill but argued for leniency, because they had comprehensive isolation procedures in place for machine operators and the worker had been retrained several times in the years before the incident.

The employer's plea for leniency was rejected, even though the offence was found to be less serious because the worker was well trained and had deliberately contravened a safe work procedure.

The legislation imposed a duty not only to provide instructions, but to ensure safe systems and machinery. The judge accepted that the worker stepped out of the boundaries of the safe work procedures and the isolation matrix, but this was an unguarded machine to which he had access.

3   OHS Alert, ohsalert.com.au

Notify serious incidents

Your business is required to let WorkCover (or your state or territory WHS regulator) know if any notifiable incidents occur as a result of your business's activities as soon as it is reasonably possible.

A notifiable incident is a serious incident that relates to your business's work and involves one of the following:

- A death
- A serious injury or illness
- A dangerous incident

A serious injury or illness is one that requires:

- Medical treatment within forty-eight hours of exposure to a substance
- Immediate treatment as an in-patient in a hospital
- Immediate treatment for a serious injury or illness such as a serious head injury, a serious burn, a spinal injury or a number of other injuries

A dangerous incident is an incident in a workplace that exposes a worker or any other person to a serious risk to their health or safety. This may include an uncontrolled escape, spillage or leakage of a substance, an electric shock, a fall from a height or the collapse of a structure.

If a notifiable incident occurs, ensure that the site is not disturbed until an inspector arrives or otherwise directs.

While only the above are notifiable to WorkCover, ensuring that you are informed of any other incidents may help your business meet its duties under the WHS Act. To this end, consider implementing a policy or procedure for reporting incidents.

Making Workers Compensation claims

When a worker is injured at work, the employer, injured worker and Scheme Agent (or insurer) each have responsibilities to ensure that the injured worker is provided with benefits and assistance to recover and return to work safely and as soon as possible. When a workplace injury occurs, the injury must be notified to the employer as soon as possible.

The employer then has a legal requirement to notify their insurer within forty-eight hours of the injury being notified. This notification time may vary based on your state legislation, so it's best to check with your local WorkCover branch. The main point to note here is that you are legally required to report any injuries as soon as possible.

Issue resolution

The issue resolution process applies after a WHS matter is raised but not resolved to the satisfaction of any party after discussing the matter. If this occurs, your business needs to follow the issue resolution process set up in the WHS laws. This information, and the process set up, can be viewed on the Safe Work Australia website at: safeworkaustralia.gov.au/sites/SWA

Provide information, training and instruction to all employees

Remember, all workers, whether permanent, casual or volunteers, must be provided with information, training, instruction or supervision so they can carry out their work safely.

Find the right consultative arrangements and consult with workers. This is compulsory. Talk about WHS matters that affect everyone in the workplace. This is a good way to ensure they are involved in the identification of hazards and the assessment and control of any risks.

Ways you might consult with your employees include:

- Write policies and safe operating procedures and develop accompanying forms together (some sample policies are in the *Resources* section of this book)

- Perform hazard inspections and determine risk assessments and controls together

- Regular newsletters, mail or email, that feature WHS news, information and updates

- Regularly update a notice board or website with information, including its latest safe work policies and procedures

- Have a suggestions email inbox for workers (including volunteers) to send suggestions to about ways to work safely and other matters

- Hold regular meetings to talk about the work they do and how to do it in the safest way

- Hold short 'toolbox talks' where specific health and safety topics are discussed

- Ensure that records are kept of consultations with workers

Health and Safety Representatives

HSRs are one way for workers to be represented in relation to WHS matters.

The appointment of HSRs is not mandatory, and an HSR is not obliged to undertake training. An untrained HSR can exercise most powers except for directing that unsafe work cease or issuing provisional improvement notices.

Your business must make possible the election of an HSR if one or more of your employees (whether paid or volunteer) ask for an HSR to be elected to represent their health and safety matters. To ensure the best representation of workers, HSRs are elected to represent specific work groups. Work groups must be determined before an HSR can be elected.

If an agreement can't be reached, there is also the option for the WHS regulator to become involved. The regulator can determine whether or not it is appropriate for there to be an HSR. If an HSR is appointed, the 2016 WHS Regulation specifies that the appointed person is entitled to attend a five-day training course and, should they be reappointed, attend a one-day refresher course. All resources, facilities and assistance must be provided to enable HSRs to carry out their duties.

Health and Safety Committees

HSCs are another way for larger organisations to facilitate consultation. HSCs are not mandatory but must be established within two months of a request to establish one from an HSR or five or more workers. An organisation can also choose to establish an HSC without a request from workers.

HSCs can assist in developing health and safety policies and procedures for the organisation.

The last word – the safety efforts of most businesses are insufficient

Every business wants to create a safe workplace, but many fail to integrate safety as a genuine guiding principle across all facets of the business. To ensure your business doesn't fall into this trap, follow these four guidelines:

1. **Don't state one thing but encourage something else**

   Too often business owners tell their workers to 'be safe, but make sure you get the job done'. This is just not on – it's downright dangerous.

2. **Safety must be driven by leadership culture, not only by a safety management system and its policies and procedures**

   The culture that leaders create – not just the policies – shapes worker behaviour. As a leader, make sure you grow a workplace culture that values positive behaviour and drives safe operations.

3. **Engage employees in the consultation process**

   The people affected by the policies and procedures *must* be involved in their development, implementation and review if they are to follow them wholeheartedly.

4. **Don't just throw training at the problem**

   Throwing training at health and safety issues fails to address the deeper cultural issues that are driving unsafe behaviour. It also sends a clear message to the workforce that leadership believes that safety is an employee issue, not a business one.

> **TIP**: If you have employees who work from home, you need to complete safety audits of their workspaces annually. Initially a self-assessment will suffice, but then you may need to move to a company-conducted physical assessment.

PERFORMANCE MANAGEMENT

I suspect that this chapter will be the one that you refer to the most. Performance management is an area that managers often find awkward – it's difficult to tell someone that they are not performing, and the process is a legal minefield – and this causes them to avoid the process rather than preparing for the difficult conversation. Instead, sub-level performance is often overlooked in the hope it might improve.

If you are in business today you need to maximise the performance of all your employees to achieve the best results. If businesses do not effectively manage their poor-performing employees, this may lead to an inferior level of client service or a poor-quality product. In turn, this can result in a loss of clients or customers, adverse publicity or exposure to liability.

Other considerations are:

- If poor performers continue to be unmanaged, it can lead to a reduction in or loss of morale for the other employees, as well as a lower standard of teamwork or a reduction in productivity

- Termination can be very expensive – it is much better to try and improve the performance to the required level. (Plus, there is also the added expense of hiring a replacement)

- The risk of an improperly managed termination may lead to a potential Unfair Dismissal claim

Strategies for managing performance

An employee should be advised of the substandard performance as soon as you become aware of it. This is a real problem because often an employee will say, 'But hang on a minute, I've worked here for five years and my work performance has never been questioned – why now?'

Once the employee is aware of the issue, they must have the opportunity to explain why their performance is lower than expected. If the employee chooses not to share when asked, 'Is there another reason that your work standards have dropped?', then you can only use the basis of the information available to decide the course of action.

If drawing an employee's attention to an issue isn't enough to change their behaviour, performance management can include some, or all, of the following:

1. **Counselling** – This usually takes place at the start of the process and where the performance issues are relatively minor. After counselling you should review the performance with the employee. It is normal for counselling sessions to occur a couple of times prior to moving to a warning stage. It is extremely prudent to document these sessions

2. **Warning(s)** – This is where the performance issue is considered more serious in nature. The need to give three warnings prior to termination no longer exists, but you do need to act fairly. It is recommended that all warnings are documented, whether the warning is written or verbal. If you have a performance warning policy in place, then you must follow this policy – if you don't, the process will be deemed to be unfair. There is no limit to the number of warnings that must be given, only that the process is fair. Obviously, the more warnings, the lower the likelihood that an unconsidered process took place. It is imperative that, prior to the final warning and termination meeting, the employee is in no doubt of the seriousness of their situation and that termination could be a potential outcome

3. **Further training or support** – This covers additional training, having a mentor allocated, regular feedback on performance or maybe the provision of some paid or unpaid time off if the performance dip is due to a personal issue

It is only after the above strategies have been exhausted that the employer can lawfully consider other options and next steps.

Conducting a performance meeting

1. Ensure that you are prepared:

   - Ensure all the paperwork has been completed as much as it can be prior to the meeting

   - Make notes to guide you to be sure that you cover everything – you should have someone available to take notes for you. Or these days you could ask the employee whether they would be comfortable with you recording the meeting and having it transcribed. This has the added advantage of being a much more accurate account of the meeting. That said, if the employee doesn't want to be recorded, you will need to revert to someone taking notes.

2. Book a quiet and private meeting space. Make sure that you have tissues discreetly available, as these meetings can be emotional. If the employee does get upset, pause, give them a moment and ask them whether they are ready to continue.

3. Book the meeting with the individual stating it is to discuss their performance and they are welcome to bring a support person along with them if they like. If they do not want to bring someone, note this for the record.

4. Explain the purpose of the meeting at the beginning and the roles of each of the participants. For example, the note taker is there only to document the meeting, the support person is there for support and can clarify questions or understanding, but is not able to defend, or respond on behalf of, the individual.

5. Walk through each of the performance issues, giving the employee a chance to respond to each. Where appropriate, and possible, provide evidence of the current performance level. For example, breakages, sales figures or number of calls taken. Ask the employee whether they can think of anything that would assist them to improve their performance. Consider all requests and then confirm what is possible and reasonable. Suggest other options to assist with the improvement if appropriate.

6. Explain the required level of performance and confirm timeframes for the required level to be reached.

7. Ask the employee if they have anything else to add.

8. Summarise the outcomes of the meeting and the next steps. If the next meeting might consider termination of employment, you must state this possibility.

9. After the meeting the minutes should be countersigned. If the employee is unwilling to do this, make a note of this fact in case the minutes are later used as evidence.

Script of an example performance meeting

You: *Sandy, I have called you in to talk about an event that I would like to understand your position on. I would also like to resolve this and move on.*

Let me tell you what I know: yesterday ABC called to arrange an order. From the phone system, I know that they were put through to you but were kept on hold for over five minutes. They requested an urgent order of tracksuits, which you were recorded as saying were in stock and that you would get them out to them that day.

Now I have received a call from ABC's MD saying that this did not happen, and they still have not got the stock. This is an issue because it makes us look incompetent and as if we don't care. As you know, ABC is a very important client to us and they have threatened to withdraw their business as a result. This would have a significant effect on our business and may result in job losses.

Can you please tell me your side of the story?

Sandy: *I don't think that they were on hold for that long, more like two minutes, and I said that I would get the order out but then it got busy and I guess I forgot. But hey, everyone does this sometimes – not just me.*

You: *Sandy, can I just make sure that I have heard you correctly – you said that they weren't on hold for five minutes, closer to two minutes, and you agree that you did tell them that you would get the order to them but that you got busy and forgot. Is that right?*

Sandy: *Yes, I suppose so.*

You: *Sandy, how do you think the client would be feeling now?*

Sandy: *I guess pretty unhappy.*

You: *Do you think that they have a right to be unhappy given the circumstances?*

Sandy: *Yes.*

You: *Sandy, have you got any ideas about how we can fix this?*

Sandy: *I could ring and apologise and accept the blame.*

You: *That sounds like a good idea. What about moving forward – do you agree that we need to avoid having this happen again?*

Sandy: *Yes, I guess so.*

You: *Sandy, thanks for your help with this today – I appreciate it.*

No one likes to have difficult conversations, but it is possible to get better at them and do them well. I have terminated hundreds of employees over the years and, as tough as these conversations are, you can do them professionally and with empathy. You need to be prepared for everything and sometimes people will surprise you. The way I look at it is that I may have done these conversations hundreds of times, but for this employee it is probably their first time and I need to be sensitive about this.

> **TIP**: Script your conversation to prepare for it. Think through possible responses and prepare your responses to these.

Performance management FAQs

1. **Can you terminate someone for poor performance?**

    Yes, and you should – but also know that many employees can turn around their performance and, if given the opportunity, will do so.

2. **Can you terminate someone because they don't fit the culture of the business?**

    No, you cannot legally terminate on a simply a culture mismatch, although typically this mismatch makes the arrangement unsuitable in the long term for both parties. That said, should the behaviours that they exhibit be contrary to the stated values of the organisation, you can manage performance on this basis.

3. **What is the process to actively manage someone's performance?**

    1. Describe the performance issue and why this level of performance is unacceptable

    2. Determine whether the employee knows what is expected of them

3. Ask whether there are any extenuating circumstances, e.g. illness of a loved one

4. Give the employee an opportunity to respond to the feedback

5. Ensure that sufficient resources, support and training have been provided

6. Agree and document the agreement in a performance improvement plan

4. Why does it often end in tears?

In many cases, there is limited performance management feedback, or conversations from the employee's point of view, before you end up in a serious conversation.

An employee should *always* see this discussion coming; it should *never* be a surprise if you are having regular check-in discussions.

5. Can they bring a friend into the performance management or termination meetings?

Yes, they may bring a support person to any performance-related discussions. This person is purely for emotional support and cannot actively respond on their behalf. If they reject the offer, make a note of the offer and the refusal and have them sign it.

6. What is the most common mistake business owners make?

From my experience, many business owners put up with bad performers and then lack the patience to exit them properly, often calling it a redundancy, which is untrue, more costly, and has implications for replacing the role within twelve months. Sometimes employees will resign at the first hint of performance management, either because they have known for some time that their performance was below par, or they just find it too confronting to go through the process.

Most business owners' reasons for termination are justified and are often supported by the FWA Ombudsman; however, not following the correct process can make it illegal.

7. Is it possible to turn people around?

Absolutely, I would say that in many cases performance can be rectified by effective communication and management. I have often heard employees say, 'but I didn't know I was doing it wrongly. If someone had just told me, I would have changed it.'

8. What does 'repudiation of contract' mean?

This is where an employer either demotes an employee or makes significant changes to their working conditions. An example would be if you were continually promising a promotion to the Head Developer role (with an increase in pay and conditions), and then you put an alternate candidate into that role. It could be argued that you repudiated the contract. The moral here is to be careful what you promise, both verbally and in writing.

9. What does 'constructive dismissal' mean?

Dismissal means that the termination was at the employer's discretion rather than the employee. Constructive dismissal occurs when it is deemed that you have left the employee with no other course of action, due to your actions or choice of words. The classic case here is where the employer says, 'resign or I will fire you.' This approach means that the employer forced the termination.

10. Can you fire someone on the spot and have them leave immediately?

Yes, if you are very sure (and have suitable evidence) that they have committed gross misconduct, that is they committed assault, fraud, drunkenness or drug use, extended absenteeism, abusive behaviour or sexual harassment, or acted in an unsafe manner. I would recommend, where appropriate, reporting this to the police. This termination would be with immediate effect and without notice pay.

11. Can you suspend someone without pay?

In most cases no (this is generally covered in your Modern Award), but if someone was accused of gross misconduct you could suspend them on full pay while you conducted an investigation. This is largely due to the presumption of innocence.

12. What should you try to avoid when terminating or dismissing someone?

The test is whether the termination was unfair, unjust or unreasonable. That is, did you follow due process and were you reasonable with your approach and expectations? For example, unreasonable criteria for improvement might be increasing billing to $300,000 revenue this month when $200,000 is a massive target – for even a top performer.

13. What is the risk if I just fire them the old-fashioned way? Or like Mark Bouris – 'You're fired!'

The risk is that the employee will put in a complaint to the FWA Ombudsman (at a personal cost of just over $70 at the time of printing), and it is highly likely you will be investigated formally with the risk of large fines, which can cover both lost earnings and an estimate of future earnings, and even be ordered to reinstate the individual to their role.

Performance management and annual reviews

Annual reviews, or performance appraisals, have been getting a bad rap recently with their value being questioned. I think that this is a little unfair because, like many processes, it very much depends on how they are being conducted, which relies on the manager and their competence.

The intention of an annual review is to provide the opportunity for a manager to review how an employee is performing and to provide the employee with constructive feedback to enable development and progression. When done well, they can increase motivation, provide an opportunity to reward individuals and reduce the need for performance management.

Where businesses come unstuck is when they feel they need to make the process overly complex, and this should not be the case. For small businesses, I recommend annual reviews during a quieter period of the year. Each employee should complete a self-assessment, which is submitted to the manager, and then the manager reviews the self-assessment and provides their own assessment. There are just four questions to discuss:

1. What have been the individual's performance strengths or highlights over the past twelve months?

2. What have been the areas for development over the past twelve months?

3. What are the areas of focus for training or development over the next twelve months?

4. What are the goals for the next twelve months? You might wish to set some Key Performance Indicators (KPIs) or SMART (specific, measurable, achievable, realistic and timely) goals here.

Then I recommend that you provide each employee with a rating:

- Does Not Meet Requirements
- Meets Requirements
- Exceeds Requirements

As a guideline, I would expect to see between 5-10% of your team in the first and last category, with the rest of your team in 'meets requirements'. Any employees falling in the 'does not meet requirements' category should, if they haven't already, be selected for active performance management.

The golden rule – be consistent

Regardless of how you deal with a performance issue, consistent performance management procedures must be followed across the business, regardless of the department in which your employee works. Employees should be treated proportionately in the same manner. You cannot fire someone for a breach of a safety process and just provide another with a slap on the wrist.

Having clear policies and processes will help ensure you remain consistent, along with reducing the likelihood of you being charged with Unfair Dismissal or discrimination.

When managing an employee's performance, all documents relating to the issue should be countersigned. If the employee refuses to sign, you should ensure a note is made of this as the documentation may be used later as evidence.

The *best practice* way of implementing an annual review process involves the following:

1. **Frequency** – Decide whether you are going to have annual or six-monthly reviews. If you choose six-monthly you might have the mid-year review as a mini review to ensure that the employee is making progress against the KPIs. The other advantage of a mid-year review is the benefit of feedback being regular and the process thereby less intimidating for all parties.

2. **Timing** – Ensure that you review your company calendar before determining a date because obviously if your busiest time of year is the lead up to Christmas, then this is not a good time to schedule reviews, even if they are the mini mid-year ones.

   Encourage your supervisors to block out time in advance in their calendars. There is never a quiet period in most SMEs when you have time on your hands to manage these processes, so you need to factor it in early and stick to it.

3. **Communication** – It is important that you have a communication strategy and templates prepared for the implementation of an annual review cycle. Be very clear about what annual reviews are and what they are not, the purpose and the outcomes expected. It can make sense to schedule the reviews prior to end of financial year and then, based on results, you might choose to allocate some pay rises for performance.

4. **Training** – It is important to ensure that your managers and supervisors are familiar with the approach, objectives, systems and the giving of effective feedback. Consider rolling out some training on the best way to deliver feedback as well as how to set KPIs or SMART goals.

   Most managers struggle to have the difficult conversations effectively, but this is a critical skill for any manager and needs to be developed.

5. **Plan** – What many people don't realise is that annual reviews can be a great opportunity to push a strategy, program of work or product by setting up KPIs to work towards the required goals. For example, to improve customer experience or reduce costs across all areas. Consider meeting with your managers to plan how you can make the combined output of the whole team meet the current goals of the business.

6. **Accountability** – Consider linking the completion of well-produced annual review documentation and meetings to pay reviews for management. I have typically found it is the same offenders who don't complete their team's reviews each time.

7. **Reflect** – No system or process in my view should continue untested or without review. Survey your team to see what they are, and are not, getting out of the annual review process and adjust it accordingly. Are there improvements or changes that can be made?

If the review achieves nothing more than thirty minutes of conversation about an individual's performance, an understanding of where they are looking to develop their career and an opportunity to say thank you, then this is time well spent.

IT ALL COMES DOWN TO COMMUNICATION

If you could improve your communication skills you would see improvements across all aspects of your business. Most people spend 70% of all their waking moments in communication. According to *People Skills* by Robert Bolton, 9% of their time is spent writing, 16% reading, 30% talking and listening is about 45%. (Although I know a few people where the listening and talking percentages are reversed).

Most problems in business can be traced back to a communication breakdown. The reasons for this are numerous such as rushed communication, inaccurate information, spin tactics, not checking to confirm understanding, or a lack of awareness of the importance of communicating effectively. The repercussions can be serious, though, and miscommunication can lead to:

- Lack of productivity
- Lack of morale
- Missed opportunities
- Safety breaches or accidents
- Unfair Dismissal complaints
- Unwanted publicity

The main issue is that employers don't think about their communication strategy when reviewing progress or conducting strategic planning. Communication does not happen as well as it can when there is no strategy behind it. Think about how and when you want to communicate with your team or employees and the format for these interactions. Your communication strategy should form part of your business plan.

Creating your communications strategy

Communication is one area where businesses let themselves down, and the reason for this is largely because is it not formally considered to be part of their overall business strategy. Like change management, communication needs to be carefully considered and planned.

Here are the aspects that you should formally consider as part of your company's overall communication strategy:

1. **Current situation** – First review the current situation and ask why you need communication. Before I go on, the answer is *you definitely do*, but consider why your business needs it specifically. The answer might be as simple as you are trying to build a culture of transparency to develop ownership and accountability.

2. **Objectives** – What are you trying to achieve through your communication? Do you want your employees to feel informed and included, and to increase their buy-in or engagement?

3. **Audience** – Who is the audience for your communications strategy? When you understand this, you may need to vary the messaging and style. For example, if the audience consisted of frontline employees, your messaging and style would be very different to how you would address an audience consisting of your Tier 1 customers. You need to understand where these groups are currently sitting in terms of their knowledge and where you want them to get to.

4. **Key messages** – What are the critical messages that you need your audience to understand? Remember, the best approach is to keep it simple, so don't try to be overly wordy or clever. Say it as it is.

5. **Activities** – This is a calendar of activities to execute the communications strategy. These need to be planned for specific events, such as an office

move, but also over the year, which may include the performance review cycle or releasing results for the financial year.

6. **Communication types** – When creating your communications strategy, consider:

- **Internal/external** – Think about the differences between how you and your employees communicate internally versus externally. Also remember that your employees may communicate externally in social interactions with people both inside and outside your business. Ensure they know what is, and what is not, appropriate to share externally

- **Informal versus formal** – There are two distinct channels of communication in businesses; formal, as in a regular meeting, and informal, as in a chat in the lift around a new product or challenge. Nowadays, office space designers are proactively trying to create spaces to encourage the informal aspects of communication and collaboration in many businesses

I recommend that you review your overall communications strategy annually as your needs and those of your stakeholders will change over time (not to mention the impact that technology is likely to have on your business and the way that you communicate).

Planning your communication

The key thing to remember is that effective communication requires planning, both for you and your employees. So, every time you have a major change or important message to deliver to your team, think about what you are going to say, to whom, when you are going to share, how the message will be shared and the outcome you want to achieve. Try and anticipate what the response will be and how you will respond to that feedback as well. Anticipate all scenarios and responses so that you are not caught off-guard and unprepared.

The best way to plan your communication is to use a mind map. I use a great tool called Simple Mind Pro. According to Wikipedia, 'mind mapping is a diagram used to visually organise information. A mind map is often created around a single concept, drawn as an image in the centre of a blank landscape page, to which associated representations of ideas such as images, words and parts of words are added'.

Use this technique to consider all the different types of information that you wish to communicate. You might like to consider financials and then branching off this you might have financial information for the accountant, for the exec team, the public and for the company. Another branch might be timing, such as end of financial year results or interim results. Another branch might be for forecasting and budgeting. There may be a branch for exceeding targets or under-performance. Yet another branch may be for reporting, and so the list goes on. Mind mapping is a great way to get information out quickly and effectively.

The channel, level of communication and detail will then vary, depending on the content and audience. Some information will have higher levels of confidentiality than other pieces.

Ways of communicating

Informal conversations

Informal conversations are the water-cooler chats or lift conversations; they make up an integral part of a business's communication web

Informal chats can do the following:

- Spark ideas or partnerships
- Identify opportunities
- Build relationships

- Spread information informally
- Strengthen inter-departmental relationships
- Solve problems
- Provide an opportunity to give feedback, both positive and negative

When informal constructive feedback does not seem to be having the desired outcome, it is time to move the feedback to a more formal and documented setting.

As a business owner, don't be so quick to break up the chatter in the kitchen as people are getting their morning coffees; instead, learn to use this channel of communication to your advantage. A word of caution here, I have witnessed that part-time employees do not tend to engage in this informal banter as they fear repercussions due to their part-time status. Encourage your part-timers to play an active role in this very important channel of communication. Lead from the front; encourage them to get involved and show support in front of full-time employees.

Formal meetings

Formal meetings can range from a complete waste of time to a conduit for success. To ensure you have an effective meeting:

- Make sure that only the people who need to be involved are invited. That means the individuals who are actively working on the project or task right now. Send the minutes or meeting summary to those individuals who just need to be kept in the loop

- Ensure that there is a clear purpose for the meeting – have an agenda

- Look to have an agenda that has the flexibility for some people to exit the meeting after their segment, rather than sitting through the entire session

- Be punctual – people should arrive on time and the meeting should start and end on time

- Take notes, including actions and outcomes

- Share the actions with the attendees after the meeting and give someone the responsibility of following up with the group

- Ensure that each and every individual knows exactly what is expected from them and by when

> **TIP**: There is nothing more annoying for employees than sitting in meetings that are poorly run when their presence was not really required. (They just happened to be on the copy and paste invite list).

> **TIP**: To ensure the meeting is really worthwhile, calculate each employee's hourly rate of pay and add them up. Did you get that amount of value from the meeting?

Enforcing these rules will result in an immediate improvement in productivity. Check in periodically to ensure that the meeting is still serving a purpose. If it isn't, bin it. Lean methodology supports the use of quick stand ups, where you literally hold the meeting with everyone standing, as this keeps it short.

Email

Email has increased our capacity to communicate *ad nauseam*, which has both benefits and challenges.

The benefits of email include:

- The ability to contact large numbers of people

- The ability to set up distribution groups

- The ability to communicate to a group, at the same time

- The ability to conduct polls and collect RSVPs

- The ability to document discussion trails

The challenges of email include:

- We don't have the capacity to deal with 100 plus emails daily

- People tend to copy in everyone, rather than think through the required recipients (plus there is often a 'cover-your-butt' mentality at play)

- The risk of communication overload causes employees to switch off and potentially miss important messages

- Individuals who have been 'blind copied' may, unintentionally, respond to everyone

Tips for effective email communication and getting the desired results:

- Craft messages carefully, clearly articulating what you want the individual to do and by when

- Use a consistent heading structure such as 'Urgent', 'Urgent and Action required', 'Read and Action' or 'For your information only'

- Adopt proactive filing and deleting protocols; having excessive data stored can be very expensive

- Only send emails to the relevant people

- Only address the email after you have finalised your content (saves embarrassing email apologies for accidental sends)

- Share email management strategies with your team

- Keep group settings up to date

Social media

Social media has forever changed the communication landscape and your ability to 'own the eyeballs' of your clients and prospects, in the words of James Tuckerman. But the best aspect of this medium is that it is a cheap way to access your clients. If you have ignored social media until now, I would suggest that you only continue to do so at your peril.

However, it does have its dark side and it is important to educate your employees about the medium. No longer is a rant over too many beers at the pub to a small group of colleagues the worst it can get. Having one too many beers and bad mouthing your employer on Facebook (to any number of people) is becoming a more common occurrence. Part of the challenge is that legislation has not yet caught up with the tsunami of social media communications and employees do not yet fully understand the ramifications of their actions. Simple aspects like Facebook owning every photo that you share, or the inability to get it back once you put it out there, are examples.

So, what are some of the dos and don'ts when it comes to managing social media in the workplace?

Don't:

- Ban Facebook. Some recent studies have confirmed that this is a very important part of employees' lives, particularly for Gen Y, and a ban could be the difference between them accepting or rejecting your job offer, or even whether they stay or resign.

- Think that all social media is bad. It can be used for good or evil. I once was speaking to the senior marketing manager of a global health organisation about the perils of Facebook. Her experience was that if anyone wrote derogatory comments on their business Facebook page, it was actually the public that would defend them. It allowed their 'fans' to do the talking. This was a much more effective response than anything the company could have said defending itself.

Do:

- Conduct annual training for your team on appropriate social media activity. Make sure that you as a business owner understand the tools, rather than burying your head in the sand. I used to think that Twitter was for people who had too much time on their hands, but Twitter has more than four million users in Australia, according to the 2018 Sensis Social Media Report and the average Twitter user follows (and comments on) five businesses.

- Confirm the amount of time that is deemed reasonable and in what circumstances your employees can access social media during work hours.

- Get your marketing team or supplier to develop a social media strategy.

- Ensure that you can monitor the sites accessed or time spent on your business equipment by your employees.

- Implement a social media policy.

Internal communication channels

Today, we are overwhelmed with a plethora of communication channels and not all are suitable for every purpose. It is important that you develop a consistent approach to selecting a channel relevant to each message. Also consider the style, tone, layout and format of the communication. People are time-poor, and you don't want to create a maze of extensive information that they have to wander through, mostly lost, searching for your message.

As an example, there can be a tendency to use email as a delaying tactic when a quick conversation would bring a situation to a speedy close. I encourage you to try to avoid email 'ping-pong' where possible. Email can be an incredible time waster, or it can be a powerful tool, when used effectively.

The following table will guide you in selecting the most appropriate communication channel for your purpose.

Choosing the best communication channel

Channel	Purpose	Audience	Benefits	Challenges
Email	Company-wide announcements or broadcast messages where a consistent and timely message is required Communicating with individuals or departments Customer or client interactions Sending weekly or daily messages from the business leader	Company-wide Individual employees Between departments Customers and clients	Ability to communicate a consistent message to large numbers	Concern around the volume of messages received, plus the importance of crafting the message appropriately
Distribution email list	Quick and easy communication between teams and/ or management Regular customer communications	All employees Customer groups	Speed and ease of communication to a specific group	Someone needs to maintain the lists
Company newsletter	Communicating non-time-constrained messages A mix of serious and social messages	Company employees	Can help to develop and maintain the company culture Can promote internal job opportunities	Can be a significant amount of work for an uncertain ROI

Channel	Purpose	Audience	Benefits	Challenges
LinkedIn group	Opportunity for start-ups to provide a private group forum for employees or consultants	Employees Customers or clients Potential candidates Knowledge experts in your field	Builds a tribe of people who know, like and trust you Building a talent pool of potential future candidates Interact with external experts in your field to stay abreast of changes or current thinking Opportunity to join groups where your clients are likely to be and then create credibility through your commentary	Requires an investment of time to interact and develop your profile
Phone call	Conference calls with multiple parties One-on-one conversations to gather information or come to an agreement Quick touch base with an employee or subordinate	Employees Customers and clients	Can get feedback and gauge reactions in real time - no waiting for an email response Can be easier to get multiple stakeholders over the phone than in the same room	Effective group conference calls need a strong facilitator to manage the call and solicit feedback from all parties

Channel	Purpose	Audience	Benefits	Challenges
Informal interaction	Catch up informally with the team at peak times in the tearoom to check in Opportunity for leaders to build relationships and influence with team members Thought bubbles, ideas or prompts often come about as a result of bumping into someone in the kitchen	All employees	An important part of building company culture, relationships, trust and the social aspect of teams	If people spend all day in the kitchen chatting, no other work is getting done
Meeting	Opportunity for debate, decision making and listening to feedback Create actions. Meetings should not be used for updates alone as this can be done by email	Project teams Departments	Can achieve a lot in a little time Ensures that projects and deliverables remain on time and on budget	Can be a waste of time for employees with little ROI if not managed well
Intranet	Employee information Used to communicate policies centrally, showcase a department or an employee, or store and share documents Broadcast announcements	Employees	A great way to share documents and manage version control	You rely on employees spending time navigating and reading the content Significant time is needed to keep the content fresh and current Someone needs to be responsible for content and updates

Channel	Purpose	Audience	Benefits	Challenges
Texting	Advise that you are running late to a meeting	Colleagues Clients	Quick and easy	Appropriate use – texting should never be used to advise that an employee is off sick, but often is
Instant messaging	Quick conversations or snippets between colleagues, e.g. 'running 10 mins late'	Colleagues	Enables multitasking Good for quick clarifications Both a positive and a negative is that it can be discreet	Can be disruptive and distracting
Google Hangouts/ Skype/ Voxer	Enable employees to talk via web cam Share screens to demonstrate information	Employees External contacts	Can make people more interactive as they are visible versus a phone call when, in theory, people can be very passive Cost-effective way of communicating (we use Voxer extensively across our dispersed team and love it!)	Some slight time delays in communication Delays when a number of people speak at once, there is often a break in the flow of conversation
Webinars	Share information with customers Excellent channel for training and development Advantage of being able to record	Customers Employees	Ensures all viewers get a consistent message Creates content that can be reused	Need to invest in understanding the tool and use of the functions, such as polls to increase interaction Can be costly

Having the difficult conversation

George Bernard Shaw once said, 'The single biggest problem in communication is the illusion that it has taken place.'

If I had a room full of entrepreneurs with teams of employees and I asked them these three questions:

1. Who has needed to have a difficult or awkward conversation with an employee? (The vast majority would put their hands up)

2. Who has avoided having a difficult or awkward conversation with an employee? (About half the room would put their hand up)

3. Who enjoys having a difficult or awkward conversation with an employee? (I would be lucky if two or three people put their hands up)

Why is this the case? Most people don't like conflict or making someone else feel bad, especially when an uneven balance of power is seen to exist. We don't get taught how to have these conversations. People react and then the conversation can go off course, and suddenly you are upset or angry, the employee is in tears and nothing has been resolved.

So, what is the definition of a difficult conversation? According to *Crucial Conversations* by Patterson, Grenny, McMillan and Switzler, it is a conversation that has 'opposing opinions, strong emotions and high stakes'.

Communication isn't always easy, so here are some tips from *Crucial Conversations* for having the difficult, awkward but very necessary conversation:

- Remember, you can control how you behave in a meeting

- Know what you want to get out of the meeting for you, for others and for the relationship

- Make sure the individual knows that you care about their goals in the conversation

- Make sure the individual feels professionally respected

- Apologise if you get something wrong

- If there is a misunderstanding regarding your purpose, start with what you didn't intend and then explain what you do intend

The best way to have a *successful* difficult conversation is to:

1. **Prepare effectively and have a suitable environment** – Take some time to document the issues that you wish to discuss and the preferred outcome. Make sure that the conversation is held somewhere private and soundproof. Acknowledge that this could become emotional and that you will need to pause and then reset if this is the case

2. **Share the facts** – Let the individual know that you want to share something important with them, that you are looking to resolve the issue and that you very much want to hear their side of the story. Discuss the facts from your side

3. **Tell them why this is a concern for you** – Let the individual know why these facts are of concern for you. What are the impacts to you? What are the impacts for the team, the business and/or your clients?

4. **Ask them to share their facts and story** – Encourage the employee to share their facts and story. Try not to interrupt but clarify if needed. If they are reluctant to talk, use silence to draw them out. If they are angry, let them know that their behaviour is inappropriate and then take a break if they need to calm down

5. **Summarise** – Summarise their point of view back to them so that they know you have listened to them. Something along the lines of, 'Just let me check that I have understood you. You have said...'

6. **Work out a way forward** – Talk about where you can go from
    here and have them agree to this. If they have suggestions that
    are suitable, look to include these

45% of communication is listening

Regardless of the format of, or the reason for, your communication,
listening will play a key part. As mentioned previously, 45% of our
communication comes down to listening skills. And I don't simply
mean 'hearing'. As Professor John Drakeford said, 'Hearing is a
sensory process by which auditory sensations are received by the ears
and transmitted to the brain. Listening refers to a more complex
psychological procedure involving interpreting and understanding the
significance of the sensory experience.'

When communicating with your employees, it is essential that you
listen to what they have to say. One part of this is getting their point
of view and ensuring you understand any feedback or grievances. But
the more significant part is checking your understanding. You might
say something like, 'Let me just check that I have understood you fully,'
before reiterating your understanding of what they said. This ensures
you're both on the same page, as well as helping the individual feel like
they've been listened to.

Another tip to help your employees to feel heard is active listening.
Active listening is where the listener is obviously involved in the
conversation. You can use verbal cues to communicate this, like, 'uh
huh', 'go on', 'okay', while physical cues like leaning forward and
nodding are also effective. Researchers argue that between 65% and
93% of all communication occurs through body language; therefore,
you need to be aware of what you are subconsciously communicating.
Try and ensure that your words and body language are in sync.

What to put in writing

According to Robert Bolton in *People Skills*, researchers claim that 75% of oral communication is ignored, misunderstood or quickly forgotten. This is why written communication is so important in the business world.

That said, what should you put in writing, and what would be more appropriate as a phone call or conversation?

When you are trying to decide what you need to put in writing versus what you can communicate verbally, think about the following:

- Does the information need to be documented?

- Will it need to be referred to in the future?

- Do you want people to have the opportunity to review it thoroughly at their leisure, so you can capture their thoughts and reactions?

- How would you feel if this information made it to the newspapers without your permission?

- Do you have a legal requirement to document the communication, for example, if it was a formal performance management discussion?

Every time you communicate with your employees you have an opportunity to influence and direct the way they behave. This is a wonderful opportunity for your business if you can capitalise on it.

MEASUREMENT – WHY BOTHER?

What is the current turnover of your business as a percentage of your total head count? Do you know? Most small- and medium-sized business owners don't.

As a guide, a healthy turnover is about 10-20%, depending on your industry. Why does this matter? Because it is damn expensive and time consuming to replace an employee if they leave! It also means you are not focused where you should be. Not only that, there will be a dip in productivity as a result while the role is vacant, which means other team members will need to pick up the slack, not great for morale or engagement.

Understanding how your business measures up against this simple metric gives you a world of insight into whether there's room for improvement, and considering how to do so.

For far too long the personnel manager has had a 'touchy feely' reputation, and this has nothing to do with being inappropriate. This reputation is fast-changing and in my view should continue to do so. At the big end of town, bit by bit, data is changing or improving the decisions made around what is often one of the most expensive costs to a business – people.

I believe that small and medium businesses need to watch, learn and take best practice from the corporate world. That being said, I believe that we can also learn from their mistakes and apply practices in a way that makes sense for smaller business owners.

Luckily, in recent years, this has become so much easier with advancing technology. The rise of Software as a Service (SaaS) has brought tools that were once the domain of the multinational right to the doorstep of every business. Big HR Information systems (here's another acronym: HRIS) have been translated into cloud-based tools that are sophisticated, intuitive and powerful. There are quite a few out there but you may want to start by looking at intelliHR (intellihr.com.au) or ELMO (elmosoftware.com.au). So how can we take these powerful processes, which were once only available to big business, and make them our own?

It starts with defining what needs to be measured, then establishing a clear framework for measuring those metrics.

What to measure

What gets measured gets managed, meaning once you start measuring, you can improve. So, let's look at what to measure.

Before we get into the detail of the different data crunches you can do, I recommend starting with the bigger picture by doing an HR diagnostic to discover the state of HR in the business – both what works, and what doesn't.

This is an absolute passion of mine; so much so that I created my own diagnostic tool, Employee Metrics (employeemetrics.com.au). With Employee Metrics, you get a high-level view of all aspects of HR in a business across the Employee Lifecycle. Employee Metrics measures potentially hundreds of touch points, assessing the level of risk and the importance of the risk to the business, and we use this to give individual recommendations for each risk identified. The tool has different levels, so you can be sure that we have a format that is right for your business. If this is of interest (and it is a great starting point for any business looking to measure their HR) get in touch via employeemetrics.com.au.

When it comes to the individual metrics that are worth capturing to enhance your decision-making ability, these include:

Headcount

Measure the number of full-time and part-time permanent employees, casuals, temps and contractors working within your business. When you're aware of the mix, you may be able to tweak it for cost savings and higher productivity.

Remember to update this with every new hire and every departure. It is important to know how many people are working for you as there may be different rules and obligations that apply for small versus large businesses.

Average salary/day rate

Tally all the salaries paid to permanent employees and divide the total by the number of employees, along with the daily salary bill (which will include casuals, temps and contractors). This is a good figure to compare to daily revenue targets.

Attrition

This accounts for employees leaving the organisation, but this can also be split into managed attrition (otherwise known as being pushed) or unmanaged attrition (legitimate resignations). Along with recording the numbers, look to understand *why* your people are leaving. There may be something that you can do to address or change this.

Vacancy costs

Another powerful piece of data is the cost to your business of having a role vacant for a certain amount of time. I know of a company that identified all its critical roles and how long these roles were usually vacant, which resulted in them identifying that these roles were vacant for 100 days on average. They then went on to calculate the resulting cost to the business, which was about $380,000 per annum. The outcome was that they started developing talent pools of these individuals to reduce the vacancy time from 100 days to a week. Now imagine what *this* is saving the business!

Recruitment costs

Another cost to review is what it costs to hire – in particular, recruitment agency fees, advertising charges and the time you invest in the team. Your time is precious, and I understand that many business owners do not pay themselves a fair and appropriate wage, rather they attempt to keep as much money in the business that they can. But think about this – the time you spend on recruitment is taking time away from activities that could be growing your business. Measuring this is the first step to making the process more efficient and reducing that expense.

Annual leave

Another advantage of keeping accurate records is that many small businesses quickly find themselves carrying a huge annual leave liability that could send them broke. Imagine if everyone took all their accrued leave at the same time, what would it cost you? I can recall one large corporate where I worked which had individuals with sixteen weeks owing, *plus* long service leave. Now, my view is that these employees would not be working to their full potential with limited rest and relaxation. This is why it's important to record and keep an eye on this and encourage employees to take their leave on a regular basis.

Make sure you review your Modern Award to see if you can close over quiet periods, such as Christmas and New Year. This can effectively reduce your annual leave balance across the business.

When monitoring annual leave, ensure you understand how many public holidays you need to take into consideration as non-productivity days. You can then work out your number of available work days by adding up all your employees' days of work minus annual leave, public holidays and, say, an average of five personal leave days per employee (knowing that some will take more and some less). This calculation will assist with any forecasting and planning requirements.

Absenteeism

Absenteeism in small- and medium-sized businesses is something that I often see being poorly managed, meaning that businesses are inaccurately accruing significantly more leave than is actually owed to employees. The big loophole here is that managers approve personal leave or annual leave and then forget to document it, while the payroll system continues to grow the balance. I witnessed a case where an employee had taken significant leave, which everyone could attest to, yet resigned with six weeks owing because there were no records to prove that he had taken this leave at all.

Engagement

Engagement is a key part of attracting top performers to your company, and in setting the conditions that encourage people to perform at their best once they are employed. Businesses that can improve their engagement scores will see positive results on the bottom line. Remember, organisations with the highest levels of engagement are outperforming others in every commercial metric, and employers with over 80% engagement experience increased productivity, customer satisfaction, customer loyalty, ability to attract and retain talent, as well as higher profits, sales and turnover. If these are not good enough reasons to pay attention to the engagement levels of your workforce, I don't know what would be.

Loss of utilisation

This is the level to which the productive capacity of a business is being used in the generation of goods and services. In this case we are looking at how effective a business is in maximising the output from employees in comparison to the salaries being paid.

Productivity measure

Productivity is a measure of the efficiency of production. It is an economic measure of output per unit of input.

While all these measures are costs to your business, they are, as well, levers that you can push or pull to reduce costs (and boost your bottom line). Music to your ears, I hear you say.

> **TIP**: Keep robust and accurate records for personal, community and annual leave.

How and when to measure?

For businesses, the easiest way to measure is probably using a spreadsheet. This does not have to be a complex spreadsheet at all. Just list all your measures and the weeks of the year, and then review each area when you are reviewing your overall company performance for the week. This employee data could be included with your P&L, sales forecast and actuals, expenses and also your employee metrics, which are typically one of your largest costs. Look to regularly review, assess and action accordingly. This could be called an Employee Scorecard.

After a couple of months of reviewing your data, it's a great idea to set some targets that you as a business want to work towards. For example, I would recommend an attrition target of between 10-20% depending on your industry (a contact centre would have a much higher attrition rate, at 30–40%). However, as long as your targets are an improvement on your current numbers, you'll be heading in the right direction.

There are a couple of key formulas that will be enough to get you started and thinking about your costs more accurately and effectively. Using these calculations will enable you to understand your numbers better and identify areas of waste. Numbers have traditionally been underutilised in the small business space yet having a handle on this data can, and will, give you a competitive edge and help you focus on areas that will give you the highest return on investment.

Attrition

The best way to measure your attrition is to first separate it into managed and unmanaged attrition.

Unmanaged attrition (resignations):

Total number of resignations in a financial year/Number of employees x 100 = Unmanaged attrition rate

Managed attrition (exits you actively manage):

Total number of terminations in a financial year/Number of employees x 100 = Managed attrition rate

Your total attrition will be the combined total:

Total number of resignations and terminations in a financial year /Number of employees x 100 = Attrition rate

Vacancy costs

A cost that businesses tend to underestimate (or lack an understanding of) is the cost of an unfilled vacancy. While it can be a relief to save the salary cost of an unfilled vacancy, the more important point is that, overall, the business is short a revenue generator. There are many ways to calculate the cost of vacancy, a simple one is:

Take the average revenue per employee:

Total revenue/number of employees = average revenue per employee

Then calculate the daily rate of revenue per employee:

Average revenue per employee/number of working days = daily revenue per employee

Then multiply this by the number of working days vacant to calculate the amount of revenue lost due to one vacancy:

Daily revenue per employee x number of days role is vacant = Vacancy cost

For example, a business with ten people that has annual revenue of $1.5 million has an average annual revenue per employee of $150,000, which converts to a daily amount of $600. So, if a role is vacant for two months, you will have lost around $25,000 in revenue. On top of this financial cost there is also the increased pressure on you and the remaining team to plug the gap.

Recruitment costs

Every employee that you lose and need to replace costs your business money. The rule of thumb calculation for the cost of replacing an employee is between 50% and 150% of their salary. For more junior roles this would be closer to 50%.

[salary x (replacement %)] = Total cost to hire

So, if you were replacing a $50,000 plus super employee who was a full-time permanent; the likely cost to the business would be $75,000, including compensation.

This calculation includes both hard and soft costs such as advertising, recruitment agencies, lost opportunity, lost productivity, and training and time for the new employee to become fully productive in the role.

To calculate the cost of the recruitment process, calculate your hourly rate multiplied by the hours involved in the recruitment process. This will include the time taken to:

- Review or write the job description
- Add the position to your organisation chart
- Write the job ad
- Place the ad on an appropriate job board or Seek
- Acknowledge all applications
- Review all applications
- Conduct phone screens with suitable candidates
- Coordinate interviews
- Interview candidates
- Advise unsuccessful candidates
- Arrange and conduct second interviews
- Make the verbal job offer
- Complete reference checks and background checks, if required
- Advise unsuccessful candidates
- Draft an employment contract

As an estimate, I would suggest that there are between fifteen and thirty-five hours of work in this process, though this does depend on the number of applications received and the number of interviews you choose to complete.

Annual leave costs

You can calculate annual leave costs by using the following formula:

Total annual leave accrued across all employees = Total annual leave liability

This figure is calculated as the number of days or weeks accrued across the business owing in annual leave.

Absenteeism measure

Absenteeism can be very expensive for businesses, especially if it becomes excessive. To calculate this use:

Average day rate salary x number of employees x number of days absent = Total cost of absenteeism

Using the day rate of $316 per day, if you have six employees off sick over one week it would cost you $9,480.

To work this back to a cost per day:

Average day rate salary x number of employees = Day rate cost of absenteeism

You can see how actively working to reduce the number of personal leave days your employees take can make a huge difference to your business. Let's say your business has twenty-five employees who all typically take their full entitlement of personal leave of ten days per annum. If we use the loss of utilisation rate as calculated above of $316 per day, this means that the personal leave component is costing you $79,000 per annum. If you can reduce this usage by two days, you will save the business $15,800 per annum. Not small numbers, are they?

Loss of utilisation

The best way to calculate this is to start with your business's average salary. The way to calculate this is to add all of your salaries and divide the total by the number of employees that you have.

Total payroll/Number of employees = Average salary

This calculation is also referred to as 'unlocking the value of a salary' and can also be calculated as a day rate.

**Total payroll /Number of employees = Average salary
/250 working days[4] = Average day rate salary**

For example, if your annual payroll is $1,350,000 and you have twenty-five employees, your average salary is $54,000. Your average day rate is $216 per day per employee.

Another way of calculating this cost is to understand, for example, how many units are produced across the business divided by the number of employees. So, then the calculation would look like this:

Number of units/Number of employees = Number of units produced per employee

To get this to a day rate of production, it would look like:

Number of units/Number of employees = Number of units produced per employee/250 working days = Average number of units per day

For example, if you produce 20,000 workstation units in a year and you have twenty-five employees, then each individual produces 800 units per year, or 3.2 per day.

Given that Australia is not performing as well as it could be in comparison to its international peers, this is a good number to understand and look to improve over time.

4   To determine the number of working days in Australia this calendar year, visit australia.workingdays.org

Productivity measure

At a company-wide level, a common calculation to measure productivity is the total revenue produced divided by the number of full-time equivalents, otherwise known as FTEs. FTEs are calculated by adding the total number of hours worked across the business (including part-timers) then dividing the total by thirty-eight hours. Typically, profit is not used for this calculation as that number can jump around a bit.

Revenue/FTEs = Productivity

As an example, say your business revenue figure is $3,750,000 and you have twenty-three full-time employees, then $163,043 per employee is your productivity measure. If your revenue stays the same in the following year and you have one fewer employee, then you will have increased productivity/employee over the year to $170,454.

Engagement costs

Employee engagement is a fascinating measure of how much employees care about their work and their company. Good research exists showing a link between high engagement and improved business results (including lower absenteeism and turnover and higher productivity and profitability).[5] This is a more complex calculation and needs to be calculated by a specialist. (See the *Surveys* information following for a quantitative and qualitative measure.)

Surveys

Some areas you might want to measure are likely to be more qualitative rather than quantitative, which means a formula won't suffice. Instead, surveys are a great way to get a sense for this type of data.

---

5   gallup.com/workplace/236927/employee-engagement-drives-growth.aspx

Engagement is one such example. One of the best tools I know for measuring engagement is Custom Insight (custominsight.com.au). This program measures how an individual feels about the business and their manager. Employees complete an online survey of sixty-three questions, taking between 5-10 minutes. The questions cover a number of different categories such as trust, purpose and direction, feedback, respect and organisational effectiveness. The great thing is that you swiftly get qualitative and quantitative data, which means you can quickly assess your three main focus areas. A benefit of having a third party conduct the survey is that your people may be more candid with their answers.

If you jump on the Custom Insight website you can get a quote, trial the surveys and see the dashboard. It works out to about $300 per employee, but the information is very beneficial.

Another engagement survey that I rate is 6Q. This simple, intuitive and easy to use tool falls more into the category of a 'pulse check' rather than the deeper dive of Custom Insight. You can set the tool to ask your team six questions on a regular schedule: weekly; fortnightly; monthly or quarterly. It takes a minute or so to complete on any device and you get a report on the results in twenty-four hours, showing results against global benchmarks and your trending results over time, giving you some great insights. There are hundreds of questions to choose from or you can write your own. 6Q is great for monitoring engagement during big change projects for instance. You can sign up for a free trial at 6q.io

If you don't want to invest in a professional engagement survey, an alternative is to run your own reviews annually. Interviews could be conducted face-to-face or by using an online survey tool, such as Survey Monkey. I believe that face-to-face surveys are more detailed, but they are time consuming. If you decide to take this route, I'd recommend that you use someone neutral questions to tease out more accurate responses.

Here are some questions that will deliver some great data on the current pulse of your business and identify any areas of concern or success.

1. What is your role?

2. How long have you worked for XYZ company?

3. What do you do to relax? Or for fun?

4. What do you like about your role?

5. What do you like about working for XYZ company?

6. What don't you like so much?

7. Across all the roles in your career to date, where has been your favourite place to work and why?

8. Describe the culture of XYZ company?

9. If you could change one thing about your role or the business, what would it be?

10. What are your career aspirations?

11. Do you see yourself at XYZ company in one year, three years or five years plus?

12. Who is your current manager?

13. Can you describe their management style?

14. Do you know where the business is going over the next eighteen months?

15. Could you please rate your level of happiness at XYZ company on a scale from 1-5, with 1 being miserable and 5 being exceptionally happy?

16. Please rate your ability to do your role in terms of systems, IT, and tools from 1-5, with 1 being impossible and 5 being easy

What are the benefits of measurement?

The challenge of measurement is the time involved in collecting, recording and analysing data, but once set up and refined I believe that this is a worthy investment of your time. Understanding your cost base, wastage, productivity and employee engagement can unlock powerful data, which will allow you to understand your business better and make more effective, timely and accurate decisions.

PART 3: EXIT

So long, farewell, auf wiedersehen, adieu…

Even in the best of companies, people move on. I remember when I worked for a large corporate organisation where the department that dealt with exits was called the Terminations Department. This always made me think of the film *The Terminator* – it comes across as a very *final* end, the point of no return. But I don't think about this process in that way. I think 'exits' is a much more appropriate term.

Regardless of the language you use, losing key employees can have a significant impact on your business, whether they resign, are made redundant or are terminated (exited). The key to ensuring the experience is as smooth as possible, for both the business and the employee, is ensuring that you have the right policies and processes in place in advance, so you know exactly what to do when an employee leaves.

RESIGNATION

Resignations are going to happen at some point in your business and when it is a great employee, it can be hard not to take it personally. Other times you might secretly be doing cartwheels on the inside. There will be instances where you see it coming or maybe another employee has warned you of the possibility. Alternately, you might have been orchestrating this outcome. Whatever the situation, there is a process and best practice that you should follow.

To avoid becoming overly sensitive to employees resigning, I think of the saying, 'People come into your life for a reason, a season or a lifetime. When you figure out which one it is, you will know what to do for each person.' Not every employee will be joining you for the entire journey. Try and work out if they are season, reason or lifetime employees and then manage and emotionally invest in them accordingly.

Verbal resignation

Typically, an employee will sheepishly – or sometimes with a look of glee – ask to see you to have a chat. They will then share the news that they have decided to resign. For many employees, this is one of the hardest conversations they will have. They may dread the experience, finding it very awkward and confronting. From your point of view, it is important to understand the reason they are resigning, where they are going and to confirm their last day.

Their last day is dependent on their notice period as per their employment contract, which is usually either one week, two weeks or four weeks. Many employees would ideally like to shorten this notice period or leave immediately. You cannot force an employee to work out their notice, although you may like to suggest that this would be in their best interest, so they leave the business professionally, reminding them that it is a small market and you might remember this aspect of their employment when you are contacted for a reference. On this point, I was recently sitting at Brisbane airport one afternoon waiting for a flight to Sydney. I looked up and recognised a fellow called Graham, who I worked for twenty years ago (ouch, it hurts me to say that, but I was very, *very* young at the time). On my last day in that role, I was the last person to leave the office because I had not yet finished something that I had committed to finishing. This must have impressed Graham as the great part of this story is that he is now a client of Employee Matters. I believe a part of the reason for this is that he remembered me for being hard working and professional, and for leaving a great impression even as I resigned.

If they can't be persuaded to work out their notice, then there are financial repercussions. For example, let's say they are required to give you two weeks' notice and they want to leave immediately. If they are paid in arrears (always a good thing to do) and it was payday today, then if they leave today you would just have to pay out any annual leave owing.

On the flip side, if they are happy to work their notice period but you would prefer them to leave immediately, you can do this. You would have to pay out their two weeks' notice plus any annual leave owing. If you have any concerns about improper behaviour or risk to the business, this is a good option. Think about the cost benefit and productivity loss before you make this decision.

Written resignation

Any resignation should be received in writing, as soon as possible after the verbal resignation. Some employees will come to tell you with a letter in hand. Some who find the conversation difficult might just slide the letter across the desk for you to read. Regardless, you do need something official in writing. All it needs to say is, 'I hereby tender my resignation effective 31 May 2019', with a date and signature included.

There was recently a case where an employee had resigned verbally in the heat of the moment and this was accepted by the employer. On reflection, the employee did not want to resign but the employer chose to complete the resignation. The employee claimed that this was an Unfair Dismissal with Fair Work, as he did not resign in writing. He said he did not mean to resign and that it was the emotion of the situation that caused his outburst. Fair Work ruled that this was in fact an Unfair Dismissal and there was an order for the employee to be reinstated. The lesson here is that all resignations should be completed in a calm manner and should be formalised in writing as soon as possible.

In the instance that an employee who has resigned (and confirmed this in writing) changes their mind, then you have a choice. If you wish them to proceed with the resignation you can advise them that this is the case. If you are happy to have them rescind the resignation, then have them put this in writing to you with the rationale, a date and signature. I would also recommend that you put a note in their file outlining the circumstances.

You would also receive a written resignation in the case of retirement, although you typically have had numerous discussions with the employee nearing retirement to understand their plans and then plan for them accordingly.

Counter offers

In some circumstances, a resigning employee could be one of your best people – someone that you really don't want to lose. In this case you may like to dig a little deeper to understand their reason for resigning and convince them to stay. The reason might be compensation, more opportunities elsewhere or a personality clash with another employee.

If you do believe that you can fix the issue and you *want* to, then put your case to the resigning employee and try to convince them to stay. That said, evidence does indicate that employees who accept a counter offer at the point of resignation often end up resigning again within six months of the original resignation, as the issue is not sufficiently addressed.

If they still want to leave then wish them all the best and stay in touch after they leave, letting them know that they will always be welcome back if they are ever interested. Sometimes employees realise after leaving that things weren't so bad after all. Re-hired employees are great because both parties know what they are getting into, they get up to speed very quickly and they tend to stay a long time the second time around.

Communication

One aspect of resignations that is often poorly executed is the communication aspect. Resignations can be extremely unsettling for the remaining employees; especially if there has been a spate of resignations recently. It is important to communicate the resignation appropriately to the broader team. An email doing this is fine, simply stating, 'Joe has resigned and will be leaving on X date. We thank him for his work and wish him all the best.' You can share some of the highlights of Joe's time with the business, which is a lovely touch because it shows both Joe and the team that you noticed his efforts and are grateful for these achievements.

Additionally, it is good practice to have a form to advise all relevant employees that an individual is leaving. This enables activities such as the termination of the IT or security access, ensuring that reception knows, or ensuring employees know how to communicate to external callers that Joe no longer works there. It is also important to organise the return of any company property, especially in this era when company mobile phones, secure ID tokens, access cards and keys are fairly common. You need to arrange for all company property to be returned on the final day. If you don't have a company asset register, you should start one to account for all property and who it has been assigned to.

In some cases, it will be very important to communicate resignations effectively to clients. Often clients can become very attached to particular team members and will feel disappointed that they are leaving, along with some concern about what this means for them. Who will look after them now? Will they do as good a job? Is there an underlying issue with the business? This is particularly important if the resigning employee is moving to a competitor because the last thing you want is for your client to walk too. Phone these clients yourself and confirm that they are important to you, that they will continue to be looked after and cared for, and that you will personally ensure this.

Another important communication aspect is to remind the individual of their obligations to your business as they leave and after they have left. This might be around client details and intellectual property which, depending on your employment contract, may continue post-employment.

Handover

Another aspect to consider is the handover for the role. You may look to have the role moved to someone else in the team or look to recruit this role externally. The handover is important to set the incumbent up for success. This is a great time to review the job description and ensure that this is still accurate. Ask the exiting employee to prepare a detailed handover document detailing everything that they do and a current status of projects or processes, plus any future possibilities that they are aware of. If they can personally hand over the role, have them complete a handover plan to ensure that all segments of the role are covered off effectively. Try to have them hand over the role and then supervise the new employee as soon as practical, because people tend to learn more effectively from doing.

Farewell

If it is a small market, the resigning employee has most likely worked hard for you and helped you build your business. It is good etiquette to farewell them appropriately. Options include a card and cake with a short speech, thanking them and wishing them well, or a lunch or Friday night drinks. Some businesses take up a voluntary collection for a gift, but this can get expensive for team members if there are a number of people leaving. I would recommend a consistent approach as your employees will quickly start to make observations and judgements if there is any disparity between farewell scenarios.

Avoiding resignations

The best way to avoid resignations is to communicate and know your team well – know what drives and motivates them and try and cater for these factors. Let them know that they can talk to you if they have any concerns. Another, sometimes more challenging approach, is to understand and embrace that not all your employees are going to be with you for the entire journey, and they are never going to share your absolute passion, drive and energy for *your* business the way that you do. Like births and death, hires and exits are very much a part of the employee life cycle and should be managed legally and effectively at all times. Remember, what goes around comes around.

> **TIP**: Remember to document everything – paper trails are critical pieces of evidence should a complaint be made against you with the Fair Work Ombudsman.

REDUNDANCY

No one wants to be in this position, but the reality is that, at some point, you are likely to have to make a role redundant. It's important for the continued commercial viability of your business to be nimble and respond to changing environments by changing your structure if required. In business today, the only constant is change and you need to be able to react and respond accordingly.

Redundancy happens when employees are no longer required for work through no fault of their own. Typically, it is either because of a financial down turn for the business or simply that the role is no longer required. But let us be very clear here – it is the *role* that is not required, not the individual. Don't be tempted to use redundancy as a disguise for not correctly managing poor performance.

Prior to the introduction of Fair Work, only employees that had retrenchment terms written into their employment contracts were entitled to any form of retrenchment payment. This was typically only in finance or professional services. Now everyone is entitled to a redundancy payment after twelve months service – unless you have fewer than fifteen employees. If you have fewer than fifteen employees, you can make the role redundant and just pay out the notice period requirements, plus any accrued leave.

The main challenge to businesses with a redundancy situation is that there is a prescribed process that needs to be followed for the termination to be deemed fair. The process is:

1. **Meeting with the individual** – Advise them that their role is at risk of redundancy and explain why this is the case. Confirm that you are looking for alternate roles within the business or group of

companies and that you encourage them to do the same. At this meeting, you should share an indicative view of the redundancy payment owing. (Remember that redundancy payments are taxed more favourably – ato.gov.au/business/your-workers/in-detail/taxation-of-termination-payments/) Send the individual home to consider their options with a document outlining the discussion.

2. **Second meeting** – Meet again with the individual a couple of days later to discuss any alternate roles for consideration. If a suitable role is found, look to move the individual into this role. If no role is identified, move to finalise the redundancy termination. Document this meeting and the payment, which is due on or before the next pay run.

How much do you need to pay?

Redundancy payments on continuous service are as follows:

Continuous service	Redundancy pay period
Less than a year	Nil
At least 1 year but less than 2 years	4 weeks' pay
At least 2 years but less than 3 years	6 weeks' pay
At least 3 years but less than 4 years	7 weeks' pay
At least 4 years but less than 5 years	8 weeks' pay
At least 5 years but less than 6 years	10 weeks' pay

Service starts from the introduction of Fair Work on 1 January 2010. So even if an employee has been with you since 2005, their service for the purposes of this calculation would only count from 1 January 2010 (i.e. four years to 2014 or eight weeks' pay). For the final payout, you will also need to include payment for the notice period and any accrued leave owing (which is annual leave but potentially long service leave also).

Also remember to check if there are any different entitlements in the applicable Modern Award. Here is a redundancy calculator to assist you: calculate.fairwork.gov.au/EndingEmployment

If you have fewer than fifteen employees, then the Fair Dismissal Code applies. (fairwork.gov.au/ArticleDocuments/715/Small-Business-Fair-Dismissal-Code-2011.pdf.aspx?Embed=Y)

Keep the future in mind

As with resignations, there may be times when you have to make a great employee redundant, and simply cannot find another suitable position for them within the company. If they are a great employee, stay in touch – they may become a future partner, client, or even re-join your company when another position becomes available. For ideas on staying in touch with past employees, refer to the *Alumni* chapter.

EXITING

If you stay in business for long enough, sooner or later you will have a situation where you need to ask someone to leave. The most common reasons for exiting an employee include inappropriate behaviour, fraud or theft, or poor performance.

As with hiring and managing your employees, when it comes to exiting, having a clear process, keeping good records, and treating all employees equally are all key to making the experience as painless as possible.

Exiting for inappropriate behaviour

Given that I have been working in HR for over twenty years I have definitely experienced some interesting scenarios. These days I'm *never* amazed at what people will do in the workplace, especially after a couple of drinks. For example...

I was at a work conference (I can see the smile creep across your face – you've been there too and have seen how some people behave) and a new joiner to the business was also there – we shall call him Hugh. It was a dress-up party and he, along with everyone else, was in character. The night began well with no indication of what was about to happen. He was reluctant to dance but seemed to be having a good time, as was everyone there. I had already gone to bed (I can't quite party like I used to!) when he finally let loose. Over the next hour, before he was finally convinced to leave the party, he had managed to:

- Push a girl on the floor and gyrate on top of her

- Dance very provocatively towards a number of uninterested girls

- Push a fellow against the wall and attempt to kiss him

- Bite a senior manager on the cheek

The trail of destruction had begun...

The next morning, I was informed of these nocturnal activities and made some discreet inquiries. On Monday, back at the office, we received a formal complaint but had already decided to investigate. The next steps we followed were:

- Hugh was called into a meeting, allowed to bring along a support person and the allegations were shared with him verbally. A written copy of the allegations was then handed to him.

- He was advised that a formal investigation was to be conducted, the process involved and that he was suspended on full pay until further notice.

- All the employees involved were interviewed plus any witnesses. All interviewees had to keep all conversations confidential (any breaches of this would also be investigated).

- We then met with Hugh again to share our findings and for him to respond to the allegations, including any reasons for his behaviour. He was also advised that he was welcome to take legal advice.

- All the interviews were then reviewed and assessed, and a determination was made as to whether the behaviour had occurred.

At this point, we needed to advise Hugh of our findings and, again, ask for a response. We advised him that the finding would be one of the following:

- The behaviour did not occur,

- The behaviour did occur but there were extenuating circumstances, or the instances were minor in nature, or

- The behaviour did occur.

In this instance, the finding was that the behaviour did occur, and Hugh was exited with notice. I have to say that Hugh was mortified but, unfortunately for him, because of the fear that some of the employees felt after the experience, and that we could not guarantee that the incident would not reoccur, the decision made was to exit him.

> **TIP:** The way to protect you and your business prior to work functions and conferences, especially when alcohol is involved, is to educate your employees on what is deemed appropriate behaviour and set clear expectations for that behaviour prior to any business event.

Exiting for fraud or theft

What to do if an employee is suspected of stealing from you

I suspect that this is a subject rarely discussed publicly among fellow business owners for fear of losing face. Other reasons include client security breaches and reputation, but I can tell you that at least 10% of my clients have experienced employee-conducted fraud, amounting to almost a million dollars. One client had a 'friend' managing the payroll for them who siphoned off $180,000 over three years. The issue was the owner trusted her – she was busy and did not take the time to check the details closely. Needless to say, they are not friends anymore. Another client runs a travel agency where an employee was writing dummy invoices and the bank details were – you guessed it – her own!

Most of us are honest individuals and we like to believe that of everyone, but what do you do if you suspect or know that someone may have their fingers in the till?

1. **Conduct preliminary investigation** – Have enough evidence to pursue a more detailed investigation and arrange to meet with them, asking them to bring a support person along. You should also have someone to make notes of the meeting.

2. **Conduct meeting** – Explain your concerns and that you need to conduct a full investigation and, while this is occurring, that they will be suspended from work on full pay. Remember that they are considered to be innocent until proven otherwise.

3. **Suspension** – Look to suspend the employee on full pay while you conduct an investigation. Check the conditions of your Award and in the future consider adding a clause in your contract to allow you to do this.

4. **Response sought** – Ask them whether they have any response to the allegations at this point and note these down. Also ask them whether there are any extenuating circumstances in play; for example, an illness or relationship breakdown.

5. **Formal investigation** – Conduct a detailed and thorough investigation until you are very comfortable that you can prove or disprove the alleged theft. This may include bank reconciliations and interviews with witnesses. Consider whether you wish to involve the police at this point.

6. **Outcome meeting** – Arrange a meeting to share the findings and suggest that they bring a support person along. Advise the outcome of the investigation and should the investigation confirm that the theft did not occur, return the individual immediately to their role and look to manage any fall out.

7. **If theft did occur** – You can exit the individual immediately on the grounds of gross misconduct without notice. Provide a letter confirming the situation and exit.

You need to manage this scenario with a high level of discretion and confidentiality before, during and after the investigation and around any subsequent exit. Ensure that you draft a communication plan for management, employees, suppliers and clients.

You should also consider contacting the police, as theft is illegal and too many employers don't pursue legal action. While this leaves the culprit without a reference from you, they still have the ability to go on to another employer and potentially repeat the crime.

You will notice that the process for dealing with inappropriate behaviour and theft are the same.

> **TIP**: Have someone who will be seen as independent conduct the investigation.

Performance exiting

It never ceases to amaze me how often I hear of non-performing employees in SMEs and the level of frustration and angst this causes business owners. I would go so far as to say that dealing with the poor performance of an employee is one of the greatest challenges for business owners. Even more surprising is, when I ask how long the employee has been a non-performer, the answer is often not days, weeks or even months – but *years*.

So why is this the case? It is because employers are confused, unsure and frightened of performance management – especially if the end result is a potential exit. One thing that I am very sure of is that, as a business owner, you cannot afford to carry a non-performing employee. The impacts can be enormous and can take a long time to repair. They often cause a loss in revenue, reputation, client relations and internal morale.

Here is a scenario that we often come across; a client calls us – quite desperate, angry and frustrated all at the same time. The employee, let's call her Rebecca, has made one too many mistakes – the limit has been reached and they can see no alternative but to exit her. The issue is that, despite numerous conversations, nothing has been documented and no formal performance management process has been followed to date. I would also suggest that Rebecca is fully aware of the fact that she is not performing at the required level, but because she has been allowed to continue on this path, it's easier for her to stay than to find another role.

But, the last straw was when Rebecca misunderstood a client brief and produced the incorrect goods, causing the business embarrassment and expense. This was not the first time and the client is threatening to withdraw their account. The business has decided enough is enough – she has to go – but how do they do this?

At this point there are four options:

1. **Rebecca resigns** – Unlikely, when she has been with the business for seven years already

2. **Rebecca's role is made redundant** – Is this a true redundancy, knowing that the business cannot replace that role for twelve months?

3. **Rebecca begins a comprehensive performance improvement plan** – Viable, but time consuming and training dollars may need to be invested in the process. Two outcomes are possible – either Rebecca returns to the required performance level or she is exited based on non-performance

4. **You conduct a 'without prejudice' or 'off the record' conversation** – Here you offer her some money to resign and to not take legal action. This offer needs to be made attractive and is a payment on top of annual leave entitlements, long service and her notice period

If you go for the without prejudice conversation, you will need to have Rebecca sign a Deed of Release, which requires that the conversation and financial offer remain confidential and that she will not take any legal action against you, either now or in the future. Also, that she will not contact clients or sully your reputation in the market (and vice versa). The challenge here is determining the amount of the ex gratia payment – it needs to be attractive enough to forgo any payment that might be awarded by the Fair Work Commission for an unlawful termination. Depending on the level of the role, salary and the likely time to find another role, this may be between one and six months of the employee's salary. (This payment is also taxed favourably, which makes it more attractive to Rebecca).

A Deed of Release separation can be a costly exit, but it can solve a problem quickly and allow you to get on with running your business and making your clients happy. We would strongly recommend that you seek legal advice on drafting the Deed of Release, as these documents are very specific to the unique circumstances of each case.

Of course, the best option is managing the performance early and recording the process, so you don't end up in this situation. For more information on this, see *Performance management* in *Part 2*.

Reducing the risk of an Unfair Dismissal claim

Any time you exit an employee for poor performance, you run the risk of being subject to an Unfair Dismissal claim, whether it's warranted or not.

To reduce the risk of an Unfair Dismissal claim, you should ensure that:

1. **You are aware of employee and employer rights and obligations**
   You can learn more about these at: fairwork.gov.au/ending-employment/unfair-dismissal

2. **The employee is aware of the standard of work expected by the employer**
   This is important to get clear during the recruitment process, both when you write the job description and when you explain the role to interviewees. While it is the candidate's responsibility to honestly

communicate their ability to perform the role in the recruitment process, it's your responsibility to conduct a thorough recruitment process – including interviews, reference checks and any necessary testing – to find the best fit. Refer to *How to find the right people* in *Part 1* for more information.

The required standard of work should also be communicated when the candidate is in the role, during their training and through supervisor feedback.

3. **A thorough, documented performance management process is followed**

    This starts with the employee being made aware of the areas where their performance is below the standard required. The employee's performance should be discussed and documented, with the employee being given the opportunity to respond to any issues that have been raised regarding their performance.

    The employee is then entitled to a probationary period to assess performance levels, and a performance assessment process is followed to identify when the standards are not being met. You must be able to show whether any inferior performance levels are objectively defensible.

    Once the area for performance management has been identified, the employee must be informed, given a chance to respond and an appropriate time to improve.

4. **You must take steps to address unsatisfactory performance**

    This may include additional training, counselling, making adjustments to the position, establishing effective two-way communication, mentoring, and ensuring regular feedback.

It is essential to show that the employee has been given a fair go.

For more information on performance management, see *Performance management* in *Part 2*.

5. **Each situation is considered carefully**

It will be difficult to defend against an Unfair Dismissal case where there are mitigating circumstances for the drop in performance, for example, illness of a partner or bullying occurring in the workplace.

A word on Unfair Dismissal and small businesses

Small businesses (those with fewer than fifteen employees) do have it a little easier when it comes to avoiding Unfair Dismissal claims.

Rather than the requirement for six months employment before Unfair Dismissal can be claimed by an employee, this requirement is raised to twelve months employment if you are a small business. Fair Work also has a checklist for small businesses to work through to ensure they have not dismissed someone unfairly. Although the requirements aren't very different to what I have described in the previous pages, it is useful if you are a small business to ensure you have covered everything on the checklist. You can find it at fairwork. gov.au/ending-employment/unfair-dismissal.

What will it cost me if I receive an Unfair Dismissal complaint?

I had a potential client contact me recently, needing some performance management support.

They had two issues. One was easy – 'Can you help us with annual reviews?' 'Yes!' I said.

The second was more complex – she had three employees who were either not performing or had poor and unhelpful attitudes. She really wanted to turn this situation around as it was having a significant impact on morale and productivity across the business. She was keen to resolve the performance issues to a satisfactory level or exit, but she was wary of the Unfair Dismissal legislation and wasn't sure what she could and couldn't do.

There is still significant mystery around the Unfair Dismissal complaints process. My main concern is that a trip to the Ombudsman is still costly, both financially and in loss of time. The reality is that it is better to not end up there in the first place.

This calculator has been developed based on significant research and practical experience and can estimate the total cost for your specific business.

For example, you might be surprised to know that, assuming your employee's hourly rate of pay is $100, and if the matter is resolved with no blame assigned to you, it will still cost you $1,650 and up to twelve hours of your time. And this is the *best-case scenario*. If the process continues and you are found at fault, costs quickly escalate. If you would like to understand the exposure you face in your business, download our calculator to find out more.

Regardless of the reason you need to terminate an employee, ensuring that you have appropriate processes in place and that you document any investigations, complaints and interactions with the employee concerned will make it far less likely for you to receive an Unfair Dismissal complaint.

DEATH

Many years ago, I worked at an organisation where an Associate Partner discovered that he had a very aggressive brain tumour. He passed away within three weeks. He went from being a healthy, happy and popular member of the team *to gone*. This was an incredible shock for everyone. This scenario is another instance when the use of an Employee Assistance Program (EAP) (*see* the section on providing support in the *Engagement* chapter in *Part 2*) would be enormously helpful for everyone affected.

An exit process needs to be managed in this circumstance, as the employment contract on the death of an employee has still been ended. The process is that you need to close off the pay and pay any outstanding annual leave or bonuses to the estate. You need to advise the superannuation company because there may also be death and disability allowance payouts due. All company equipment needs to be returned and all logons and access to IT systems need to be deleted. In addition, you need to carefully manage the communication to both employees and clients. You might need to arrange for special leave for employees to attend the funeral.

The estate of the deceased employee is entitled to all outstanding wages and annual leave. There might also be some long service leave entitlements, which you can check with the appropriate state legislation. Superannuation will typically go to the nominated benefactor directly or the estate. When a person dies, their assets are frozen until the relevant documentation has been received, so it is important for you to wait until this documentation is received before paying out to the estate. You should hear from the Executor of the Estate providing evidence of his appointment and requesting funds owed to be paid into the account of the Estate of the Deceased.

There may be a requirement to manage the return of company assets but this, of course, needs to be managed at an appropriate time and very sensitively, given the circumstances.

EXIT INTERVIEWS

Just recently, a client of ours had a senior member of the team resign and they asked us to conduct an independent exit interview with the employee. If you're like most small business owners, you might ask why. (You might also say, 'Good riddance!' or 'What's the benefit of *that*?')

Well, I'm glad you asked:

1. **Recruitment** – In the case above, the employee had faced some challenges in the role. Before recruiting for this role again we were able to obtain detailed information that would help us recruit the best possible candidate for our client.

2. **Information** – Employees are generally more forthcoming when they have resigned. You often find out gems of information that would otherwise be withheld. Is this perhaps an opportunity to restructure the team or reduce headcount for a low cost?

3. **Rehire** – Have you ever lost an employee that you wished you hadn't and wished you could get them back? An exit interview is an opportunity to reiterate the fact that should they ever wish to return they are welcome to approach the business to see whether there is a suitable role available. People need reassurance after resigning to ensure that there are no hard feelings or misunderstandings.

4. **Stats** – Why is your team leaving you? Is there one team or area that has particularly high turnover? Is this telling you that there is another bigger problem that you need to deal with to stop the drain of skills and talent? Remember, healthy, unmanaged attrition should be between 10-20%.

5. **Alumni** – Ex-employees can become future clients, advocates for your business, rehires or just great sources of information. Take a longer-term view of the resignation and the opportunities it might bring, rather than the gap it creates.

You should have someone other than the direct manager complete the exit interview – ideally a manager from another team or division. You should have set questions, so that you can develop data over time for analysis.

What to ask in an exit interview

If you aren't sure where to start, here is a copy of our exit interview template:

EXIT INTERVIEW	
Employee name:	Title:
Reporting to:	Title:
Interview date:	Exit date:
Length of service:	
What is your main reason for resigning?	
• Compensation • Better role • Conflict with colleague • Travel requirements • Distance travelled to work • Lack of opportunity • Lack of promotional opportunities	• Culture • Lack of training • To return to study • Moving interstate/ overseas • Headhunted • Other, please specify?
What is your secondary reason?	
What have you enjoyed most about your time at [company]?	
What have you enjoyed least about your time at [company]?	
How would you describe the culture at [company]?	
Do you know what the company core values are? What are they?	

Do you believe that the company lived their core values?
How would you rate the management team at [company]?
Poor ☐   Average ☐   Good ☐   Excellent ☐
How would you rate the training at [company]?
Poor ☐   Average ☐   Good ☐   Excellent ☐
Would you recommend working at [company] to your friends? Yes/No. Please explain
Where are you going to work (if applicable)? What appealed to you about that role?
Would you be interested in joining our alumni program (if applicable)?
Can you please confirm an email, postal address or phone number, so that we can pass on any communication?
Have you returned all company property yet? If not, what is still outstanding and when can we expect this to be returned?
Please sign acknowledging that this is an accurate account of our interview.   Signed: Interviewer: Date: Date:

Exit interview data can be a very beneficial source of information for a company and is relatively easy and inexpensive to gather. I would recommend that you prepare a spreadsheet to capture all the data and then you can start to identify trends over time. Sometimes clients see that there is an unusually high exit rate from a particular team. Remember, employees leave managers, not organisations. The best course of action in this instance is to conduct one-on-ones with the remaining team members to ask them a series of questions such as:

- What do you like about your role?
- What do you like about working here?
- What would you change if you could?
- Is there anything that you don't like?
- Confidentially, is there anything that you think that I need to be aware of that maybe I am not?

Another common trend is when a number of employees leave for compensation reasons. If this is happening, you need to understand how your pay rates compare with the rest of the market. You should be aware of this data, regardless. It doesn't mean that you have to be paying in the ninetieth percentile, but you do need to know where you are currently positioned in the market. At a minimum, you need to pay the minimum Award payment; however, most employers will typically be paying in the fiftieth to seventy-fifth percentiles.

Remember it is not all about compensation – there are many other reasons why people leave. An exit interview can help you discover these.

ALUMNI

Employees will inevitably leave your business from time to time for a variety of reasons. It is important that you create a culture and environment where people enjoy coming to work and are reluctant to leave. That said, people do move away or decide to take an extended break – they might want to raise children, or they may get an offer from elsewhere that is too good to refuse. Given how difficult it is to find quality employees, it makes enormous sense to run an alumni program. This is an opportunity for the ex-employees of your business to stay connected and to be kept current with the business and its progress. It is not uncommon for an ex-employee to become a future client, to recommend your business, or to even get re-hired down the track. They could also become an advocate for you and your business, sharing leads or increasing your network with important contacts.

It is relatively simple to run an effective alumni program with the assistance of modern technology. You might email ex-employees (with their permission, of course) with updates or you could set up a locked private group on LinkedIn and interact that way. You need to communicate on a quarterly basis (as a guide) and share what is happening in the business through your alumni newsletter. You will need to ensure that you maintain your alumni's contact details (ensuring their privacy is not compromised) and you can initiate this process at the end of the exit interview. It should be stressed that the program is totally voluntary.

Many organisations hold annual events where ex-employees can socialise, reminisce, and share stories and leads.

How to create an alumni program:

1. Promote the program as a positive initiative and an extension of the organisation itself.

2. Talk about it when your employees first join the company.

3. When conducting the exit interview, raise the subject of the program again and ask whether the individual would be interested in joining.

4. If not, let them know that if they ever change their mind they are welcome to join later.

5. If they agree, update the alumni program participants register to ensure that they receive the alumni newsletter and notification of any relevant events.

6. A week after the individual has left the business; send them the alumni welcome email to ensure they know they have been added to the register.

Accenture, one of the largest management consulting companies in the world, is a good example. Traditionally Accenture had an up-or-out philosophy, but the alumni program has allowed highly valued ex-employees to remain close to the business. This network has become extensive and tight-knit, and there is significant additional business done as a result that may not have occurred otherwise. They can rehire employees very cost effectively and often their ex-employees become clients who are already 'pre-sold' on the value that a company like Accenture might bring to their current employer.

Additionally, when individuals have had a good experience at an organisation they are much more likely to spread positive stories about the business. Free press, if you like.

WHAT'S NEXT?

The impact of an employee leaving a company is often only felt once they're gone. To lessen the impact, you need to consider what happens once they've walked out the door. Do you need to hire a replacement? Is there a suitable replacement in the business, or will you have to look externally? Or can the role be absorbed into some existing positions?

As always, start by revisiting your organisational plan.

Phase 1 – Organisation charts

1. Review your organisation chart. Where did your former employee sit, to whom did they report, and what was their level of responsibility?

2. Consider, does their role still make sense? Can it be merged with someone else's role, or does it need to be split into separate areas? Also consider your business plan and how your business might need to look in future to continue servicing your clients – is this role still relevant in the future scenario?

3. Update your organisation chart to accommodate how this role will need to look in the future – whether that's the same as it was, a part of someone else's role, a new role, or several new roles. This will be your roadmap when it comes to hiring their replacement.

Phase 2 – Job descriptions

1. Pull out the original job description for the role – is it still current or does it need to be reviewed?

2. Update the job description now, including updating any existing roles that changes to this role will impact, along with new roles that need to be created.

Phase 3 – Transition plan

1. Plan how you will transition the new role in the business. Whose roles will change? How many roles have been created? Who is going to pick up the slack while you recruit someone new? Do you have a handover document in place?

2. If any management positions are available, look to your existing employees to see whether there's anyone you can promote or give extra responsibility to – refer to your 'stars' from the version of this exercise in *Organisational development* in *Part 2*.

3. If there is no one suitable among your existing employees, return to *Part 1* to begin the recruitment process for someone new.

CONCLUSION

When I started this book, I wanted to share my knowledge to help businesses in Australia to be the best that they could be. I could see that many businesses were missing the critical element or lever that could massively impact their success – and their employees. But more importantly, it was about their team, their people. Most people who work in SMEs do so because they crave the ability to make a difference, rather than just being another number. I wanted owners and managers to see themselves as a critical piece of the puzzle and become leaders that their employees respected, admired and even loved.

It was also about using the best practice that I had learnt from my corporate experience and applying this in a practical way that made sense for small businesses. My thinking is that we can leverage the millions of dollars that large corporates invest in employee relations to give us a competitive advantage.

My hope is that this book helps a business hero every day as they work through the complicated employee relations space and manage complex relationships with employees. I want this book to become a dog-eared companion of a business owner or manager sitting on their desk, helping them when ten minutes before a meeting with an employee over a performance issue, they can refresh their memory on the best process to keep them well away from the Fair Work Commission.

There is one last secret that I must share, which is a critical piece to this employee puzzle. That is the need for ownership and accountability. You must assign someone to own each aspect of this book (if it is not you) that you implement. If you don't, *nothing will happen, and nothing will change*. Implementing the strategies suggested in this book will make an enormous difference to your business and your employee engagement levels.

To continue to get advice on how to get the most out of your employees, contact me at natasha.hawker@employeematters.com.au or join our monthly newsletter at employeematters.com.au/contact/, which includes updates on changes to legislation that will impact you and, more importantly, the action you need to take as a result; webinars and videos with practical tips to apply to your business today; as well as templates and checklists you can use in your employee management.

From employeematters.com.au you can download our free eBook *Winning the War for Talent* and complete the Employee Metrics diagnostic (employeematters.com.au/employee-metrics-mini/) to see how you are positioned in the employee space, in terms of your current levels of HR compliance, risk and best practice.

Finally, please reach out to me on social media to share your stories and successes after reading this book. You can contact me on the following channels:

Connect with me on LinkedIn: linkedin.com/in/natashahawker

Follow me on Twitter: twitter.com/NatashaHawker

Like us on Facebook: facebook.com/Employeematters

Follow my blog: employeematters.blogspot.com.au

You might also like to sign up for our newsletter where we share short video tips you can apply immediately in your business, great articles and checklists at employeematters.com.au/newsletter-subscription/

Also, as a special deal for readers of *From Hire to Fire*, if you contact Employee Matters and choose us to help you with your:

- Employee Metrics SME or Enterprise
- Employee policies
- Recruitment
- Redundancies
- Termination of a non-performer
- Appropriate workplace behaviour training
- Compensation and benefits audit
- Investigation

Or you purchase the online Hire to Fire Toolkit and subsequently become a client; share the code FHTF2018 for 15% off your first invoice.

Lastly, when I was starting out in business, a dear friend of mine, Kara-Lee Richards from Precise Value, said that owning and running a business is, 'Like a roller coaster with huge ups and downs and you just need to hang on and enjoy the ride'. I hope this book helps you smooth out some of the dips and makes for happy riding.

RESOURCES

SAMPLE INTERVIEW QUESTIONS

Technical – Can they do the job? What skills are they bringing to the role?

- Ask the candidate to talk you through their CV, talking about areas of responsibility, achievements, challenges, the culture of their previous organisation, their management style or, alternately, how they like to be managed and their reasons for leaving their last position.

- Ask them technical questions about their relevant field of work and qualifications:

  - What can you offer us?
  - What are your strengths?
  - What are your limitations?
  - What are your ambitions for the future?
  - What motivates you in the workplace?
  - In what previous role, did you feel the most motivated and why?
  - What do you know about our company?
  - What is the most attractive aspect of the role we are discussing?
  - What is the least attractive aspect of the role that we are discussing?
  - What do you look for in a job?
  - What hours have you been used to working?
  - How long would it take you to make a meaningful contribution to the business?
  - What is your management style?

- How do you like to be managed?
- Why do you feel that you have the potential to be a good manager?
- As a manager, what do you look for when you are recruiting your employees?
- If you were presented with this technical problem – xxx – what would you do?
- What important trends do you see coming in our industry?
- Describe your ideal working environment.
- Looking back on your past employers, which was your favourite employer and why?
- How much financial responsibility have you had in the past?
- How many people have you supervised in the past?
- How do you think your direct reports perceive you?
- How do you think your peers perceive you?
- In your most recent role, what were some of your most significant accomplishments?
- Why have you not found a position after these many months?
- What did you think of your previous boss?
- What do you like better: working with figures or with words?
- Describe a time when your work was criticised.
- If I spoke with your boss, what would they say are your greatest strengths and weaknesses?
- How do you handle pressure?
- If we were to offer you this role, what salary would you be seeking?
- What other roles are you considering currently?

- What sort of reading do you do?

- What do you like to do on the weekend?

- Are you a leader? Why do you think that?

- How long would you expect to stay with our company?

- Are you continuing with your education?

- What personal accomplishments are you most proud of to date?

Behavioural – How do they work?

- As a manager, have you ever had to terminate someone?
  If so, what were the circumstances and how did you handle it?

- Tell me about a time when you were technically challenged.
  What happened? What did you do?

- Tell me about a time when you were likely to miss your forecast.
  What happened and what did you do?

- Tell me about a time when you had more work than you could
  handle. What happened and what did you do?

- Tell me about a time when you led a project.
  What happened and what did you do?

- Tell me about a time when you helped increase sales or profits.
  What happened and what did you do?

- Tell me about the most difficult customer that you have had to deal
  with. What happened and what did you do?

- Tell me about the most satisfied customer that you have had.
  What happened and what did you do?

- Tell me about a time when you were under excessive pressure.
  What happened and what did you do?

Cultural – Are they likely to be a cultural fit to the organisation?

- Tell me about a time when you worked for an organisation where you struggled with the culture. Why was this the case?

- What type of culture works best for you and why?

- As a first impression, can you describe the culture you see or feel here?

- What is a personal value of yours and why is it important to you?

- One of our company values is integrity. Can you please tell me about a time where you have had to live this value in a previous role?

Probing – Can you get more information?

- What area was your role in?
- What did you do?
- What did you say?
- What were you thinking?
- What were you feeling?
- What happened next?
- If you had your time again, would you do anything differently?

Summarise at a very high level what you have heard to ensure that you understood the content and to show the candidate that you were listening.

Questions to avoid

- Chain or multiple questions – What do you think?

- Leading questions – If you were leading a team and we needed you to fire some people, would you?

- Multiple choice – When you led the team did you:
  1. Lead by example,
  2. Hide in your office, or
  3. Outsource management of your team to your 2IC?

- Questions using excessive jargon – Do you know how to do a SOAP for HRLT for the next SOP meeting?

- Assumptive questions – So, you were solely responsible for that outcome.

- Closed questions, which only require a yes or no. Sometimes you need to use these to proactively control a candidate, particularly if they are overly verbose. Using a couple of control questions will quickly regain control of the interview, such as, did you finish high school? Did you go to Sydney Uni?

- Questions that could be interpreted as discriminatory:
  - What childcare arrangements do you have?
    Rather, pose it as 'It is sometimes necessary to stay late at short notice, would you be able to do that?'

  - Does your religion prevent you from working on certain days of the week? Rather, pose it as 'Ideally we are looking for someone to work Monday to Friday 9-5pm. Would you be able to work these hours?'

  - What does your disability prevent you from doing?
    Instead ask 'Are there any adaptations to the work environment that would assist you?'

SAMPLE POLICIES

Annual leave

Purpose of this policy

[Company] is committed to providing a supportive environment for employees. Therefore, all permanent employees are entitled to annual leave.

Definitions

Annual leave – The number of days of paid leave for holidays after a period of continuous employment.

The policy

Annual leave is usually an allowance of twenty days for permanent full-time employees, per annum. Part-time employees are entitled to leave on a pro rata basis, based on their proportion of ordinary hours worked. There is a provision for employees to be paid out their accrued Annual Leave entitlements on termination.

The length of this leave is to be agreed between [Company] and the employee. Employees should request Annual Leave in writing which may or may not be approved. Employees should provide as much notice as practical of the intention to take Annual Leave. [Company] must have reasonable grounds for refusing a leave application.

[Company] may request that Annual Leave be taken, provided that the requirement is reasonable and that a reasonable notice period is given. [Company] may also require employees to take Annual Leave during an annual close-down if this is deemed reasonable. Where an employee does not have sufficient leave to cover the annual close-down, the employee would be allowed to take the leave in advance.

An employee may be terminated while on Annual Leave but only for a legal reason such as redundancy, summary dismissal or where the employee has repudiated their contract.

[Company] can replace the employee temporarily with another employee but the replacement should specifically be made aware of the temporary nature of the role. On the return of the employee they should be returned to the same position, responsibilities and seniority.

Generally there are no restrictions against an employee working for another company during their Annual Leave as long as the employment does not pose a conflict of interest.

Employees are entitled to be paid out all accrued Annual Leave entitlements upon termination or death.

Approvals and review

Policy review date:	22 October 2012
Policy approved by title:	Managing Director - [Company] Pty Ltd
Policy approved by signature:	

WHS Policy 1 – Master Workplace Health and Safety Policy

Purpose of this policy

Health and Safety at work is both an individual and shared responsibility of everyone at [Company].

This policy confirms our company commitment to providing a safe working environment for all employees, coordinators, volunteers, contractors, and visitors to our workplace(s), and to provide effective communication about Workplace Health and Safety (WHS) matters.

The policy

[Company] is committed to providing a safe and healthy working environment for employees, volunteers, contractors, visitors, and all other persons whose health or safety could be at risk through our work. We will do this by ensuring:

- compliance with relevant legislation, including the WHS Act and supporting regulations

- the implementation of the Work Health and Safety Management System, and the reports, plans, policies, procedures and programs necessary to support and implement this policy

[Company] accepts responsibility for implementing and maintaining this WHS Policy and WHS Management System. We will ensure that:

- We establish measurable safety performance objectives and targets and that we review these to continuously improve WHS performance. This shall include regular workplace inspections and the prompt control of identified hazards.

- Employees and volunteers are trained on all health and safety matters relevant to their work.

- Contractors are fully aware of the hazards associated with their work, and implement appropriate hazard control measures.

- All managers, coordinators, employees, volunteers, contractors and other persons are inducted into the requirements of the WHS Management System, and are held accountable for enacting their roles and responsibilities as defined in the WHS Management System.

- Effective employee, volunteer and contractor consultation on health and safety matters includes the two-way communication of relevant information, meetings, reporting and feedback mechanisms.

- Adequate resources are provided to enable full implementation of this WHS Policy and WHS Management System. Where [Company] does not have the necessary in-house knowledge or expertise to enable it to meet its Work Health and Safety objectives, it will ensure that advice and guidance are obtained from a competent WHS professional.

- This WHS Policy and the WHS Management System are reviewed every year to ensure they remain relevant and appropriate to [Company].

All directors/officers, employees, volunteers and contractors at [Company] are required to comply with this WHS Policy and the WHS Management System at all times. The directors/officers are responsible for the implementation and dissemination of all matters dealing with the health and safety of employees, volunteers and contractors under their control.

Employees, contractors and volunteers must cooperate with [Company] regarding safety actions taken to maintain health and safety. In addition, they shall take reasonable care of their own safety and not adversely affect the safety of others at the workplace.

This WHS Policy shall be posted in the [Company] workplace at all times.

Approvals & review

Policy review date:	
Policy approved by title:	[Company] Pty Ltd
Policy approved by signature:	

WHS Policy 2 – Safety Duty Holders

Purpose of this policy

All [Company] personnel are required to ensure that the promotion of a safe work culture is evident in all that we do.

Such a culture is achieved by each of us playing a contributing part. The sum of our efforts combines to create the culture.

Policy

Designated duty holders at [Company] are established under the Work Health and Safety Act 2011.

Duty holders are made aware of their obligations under the above legislation and ensure that they fulfil these obligations (to follow) at all times.

This policy defines who the safety duty holders are at [Company]. The safe operating procedure (to follow) outlines what they must do to comply with their safety obligations when implementing the above processes.

The WHS Act imposes obligations on three critical levels of duty holders in the [Company] workplace. The levels are:

Officers (Directors)	Duty to exercise their duty-of-care diligence
PCBU	Duty to do what is (the organisation i.e. [Company]) reasonably practicable
Workers	Duty to take reasonable care and comply with reasonable direction (inc. contractors & volunteers)

Directors/Officers:

[Company] officers are required to exercise their due diligence duty at all times, to ensure that the organisation complies with its safety obligations. The directors/officers at [Company] include:

_____

_____

_____

_____

_____

_____

Person Conducting a Business or Undertaking (PCBU):

As a 'person conducting a business or undertaking' [Company] is required to exercise its duty to take all reasonably practicable steps to ensure the health and safety of workers and other persons impacted by the business. Persons representing the PCBU at [Company] include:

_____

_____

_____

_____

_____

_____

Workers:

[Company] workers, including contractors and volunteers, are required to exercise their duty to take reasonable care for their own health and safety while at work, and to take reasonable care so that their conduct does not adversely affect the health and safety of other persons at the workplace. The workers at [Company] include:

_____

_____

_____

_____

_____

_____

Approvals & review

Policy review date:	
Policy approved by title:	[Company] Pty Ltd

WHS safe operating procedure – Safety Duty Holders

To build the culture described by WHS Policy 2, we must affect and implement certain key safety functions and operations.

The ideal duty holders of these functions or operations are shown in brackets. However, responsibility for their implementation may be shared, the resulting arrangements must be communicated effectively to all, and overall responsibility retained by the directors/officers.

The functions and operations include:

- A demonstrated commitment to safety by the directors/officers (directors/officers)

- Demonstrated workplace safety consultation processes (directors/ officers, PCBU, workers)

- A WHS Management System which enables the effective management of risk (directors/officers, PCBU, workers)

- An ongoing program of safety training and supervision (PCBU)

- A documented method for reporting safety (directors/officers, PCBU, workers)

- Notification of incidents (directors/officers)

- Established arrangements for Workers Compensation and return to work (PCBU)

[Company] Safety Duty Holders – Practical ways to meet our duties:

1. Directors/officers

Directors/officers demonstrate their safety due diligence by the development and implementation of a WHS Management System that strengthens their:

- Full understanding of the business,
- Development of a safety culture, and
- Safety resource allocation.

[Company] directors/officers must be proactive and visible health and safety leaders. They may delegate tasks but not their responsibilities under the WHS Act.

2. Person conducting a business or undertaking (PCBU)

As a PCBU, [Company] directors/officers have a concurrent duty to take all reasonably practicable steps to ensure the health and safety of workers and other persons impacted by the business or undertaking.

'Reasonably practicable steps' means those available ways of eliminating or minimising the risk of injury having considered a number of relevant matters together, such as the likelihood and severity of the risk and the means to control it, weighed against the costs associated with eliminating or minimising the risk.

This includes ensuring that the workplace and anything arising out of it are without risks to health and safety.

3. Workers

[Company] workers and contractors must comply with reasonable directions and instructions as well as cooperating with any reasonable policy or procedure by the directors/officers.

Approvals and review

REFERENCES

Long service leave

ACT	accesscanberra.act.gov.au/app/answers/detail/a_id/3008/kw/long%20service%20leave#!tabs-2
NSW	industrialrelations.nsw.gov.au/Employment_info/Leave/Leave_calculators.page
NT	workplaceadvocate.nt.gov.au/pdf/NT_LSL_Act_FAQ.pdf
QLD	business.qld.gov.au/running-business/employing/employee-rights/long-service-leave
SA	safework.sa.gov.au/law-compliance/compliance-rights/wages-conditions/long-service-leave?id=2477#
TAS	worksafe.tas.gov.au/laws/long_service_leave
VIC	business.vic.gov.au/hiring-and-managing-staff/long-service-leave-victoria
WA	commerce.wa.gov.au/labour-relations/long-service-leave-0

Work Safe

Work Safe Australia	safeworkaustralia.gov.au/
Safe Work NSW	safework.nsw.gov.au/
SIRA	sira.nsw.gov.au/
icare	icare.nsw.gov.au/
NT Worsksafe	worksafe.nt.gov.au/
Workcover QLD	worksafe.qld.gov.au/
Workcover SA	safework.sa.gov.au/
Workcover TAS	workcover.tas.gov.au/
Work Safe VIC	worksafe.vic.gov.au/
WorkCover WA	workcover.wa.gov.au/

Other websites to refer to regarding Worker's Compensation

safeworkaustralia.gov.au/statistics-and-research/statistics/fatalities/fatality-statistics

safeworkaustralia.gov.au/statistics-and-research/statistics/disease-and-injuries/disease-and-injury-statistics

safeworkaustralia.gov.au/doc/comparison-workers-compensation-arrangements-australia-and-new-zealand-2016

Workers Compensation Act 1987 Sect 155 & Sect 156

Visas and sponsorship

Department of Home Affairs	immi.gov.au/Pages/Welcome.aspx
VEVO	immi.gov.au/Services/Pages/vevo/vevo-overview.aspx
Migration	We recommend: Patrick Vanderham (hemispheremigration.com.au) Registered Migration Agent MARN 1569037

GLOSSARY

Annual leave – Holiday leave that is accrued by permanent employees which is typically up to four weeks per year.

Background check – Where you verify qualifications, academic records, credit record or criminal history.

Casual employee – Where an employee is paid a higher hourly rate as compensation for the role not being guaranteed and the work is irregular by nature.

Change management – The management of changes within a business.

Culture – Personality of a company from a vision, values, norms, systems, symbols, language, assumptions, beliefs and habits perspective.

Department of Home Affairs (DHA) – The Department manages visas, immigration control, citizenship, ethnic affairs and customs and border control.

Duty of care – A moral or legal obligation to ensure the safety or wellbeing of others.

Employee Assistance Program (EAP) – A counselling support program provided by employers to support their employees and usually their families during difficult times.

Employment contract – A formal agreement that sets out the terms and conditions of the employment arrangement.

Employee engagement – The measure of an employee's willingness to provide discretionary effort.

Employer Nomination Scheme (ENS) – Allows Australian employers with a business located anywhere in Australia to sponsor overseas skilled workers for permanent residence to fill skill shortages in their businesses.

Equal Employment Opportunity (EEO) – Eliminating barriers to ensure that all employees are considered for the employment of their choice and have the chance to perform to their maximum potential.

Fair Work Australia – Fair Work Australia is the Australian Industrial Relations Tribunal.

Fair Work Commission (FWC) – The National Workplace Relations Tribunal is responsible for, among other duties, facilitating in good faith bargaining.

Fair Work Information Statement – Part of the National Employment Standards and sets out the minimum requirements for all employees covered by the National Workplace Relations Commission.

Fair Work Ombudsman (FWO) – The Fair Work Ombudsman has the role of educating and enforcing Australian Workplace laws.

Independent Contractor – A person, business, or corporation that provides goods or services to another entity under terms specified in a contract or within a verbal agreement.

International English Language Testing System (IELTS) – International English Language Testing System assesses the English language proficiency of people who want to study or work where English is used as the language of communication.

Job brief – Where you gather information on the attributes that a business is seeking for a job vacancy.

Jury duty – Where an individual is required to serve as a juror in legal proceedings.

Long service leave – Additional paid leave which employees can access after ten years of service. The amount of leave varies between states.

Mandatory Data Breach – Legislation that requires Australian businesses that have been affected by a serious data breach to notify all customers whose information may have been compromised.

Modern Award (Award) – Industry or occupation-based minimum employment standards which apply in addition to the National Employment Standards.

National Employment Standards (NES) – Ten minimum terms and conditions of employment.

Organisation chart – A visual representation of an organisation's structure.

Orientation – The formal integration program into a new place of work.

Parental leave – Where an individual can take paid and/or unpaid leave to care for children.

Performance appraisal – A review and discussion about the performance of an employee.

Performance management – Where an employee's performance is below the performance levels required and is being actively managed.

Permanent employee – Where an employee works for an organisation with a view to a long-term relationship and where the employee receives benefits such as sick leave, long service leave and parental leave among other benefits.

Personal leave – Otherwise known as sick leave, which can be used for an employee's illness and also their immediate family.

Privacy Act – Regulates the handling of personal information about individuals. This includes the collection, use, storage, access to, correction of and disclosure of personal information.

Professional Indemnity – Insurance for professionals who provide advice or a service to their customers.

Public Liability – Insurance to cover your legal liability when you are found to be legally responsible for damage or personal injury to a third party.

Reference check – Where you verify previous experience, job role, activities, length of service and performance.

Superannuation – Regular payment made into a fund by an employee to help them fund their retirement

SWOT – An analysis of an organisation's strengths and weaknesses, as well as its external opportunities and threats.

Unfair Dismissal – When an employee is dismissed from their job in a harsh, unjust or unreasonable manner.

Visa Entitlement Verification Online (VEVO) – *A* free online service that allows visa holders and registered Australian organisations to check the details and entitlements of a visa.

Volunteer – Where an individual works for an organisation without being paid.

Workers Compensation – Insurance to cover loss of income and payment towards medical bills where an employee is injured at work.

Workplace Health & Safety (WHS) – Workplace Health and Safety, the area that covers everything relating to the health and safety of employees, contractors, volunteers and the public in the workplace.

Workplace right – 'Includes the right to a benefit, a right to participate in proceedings or generally the ability to make a complaint or seek an inquiry under a workplace law or workplace instrument.' (Australian Master Human Resources Guide – 7th Edition 2009)